U.S. Marine Corps Unit Ingnia in Vietnam

I0809089

U.S. MARINE CORPS UNIT INSIGNIA IN VIETNAM 1961-1975

A PHOTOGRAPHIC REFERENCE

E. Richard Wilson III

Schiffer Military History
Atglen PA

Dedication

To my wife and friend Julia; my daughter Katelyn, my grandson Terrence, and granddaughter Heather

and in loving memory of

Leo Willard Povick and Nicholas Michael Povick
They will be sorely missed and live on in my heart

Copy Editor Julia Ann Wilson

Book Design by Ian Robertson.

Library of Congress Control Number: 2003114190

Printed in China.
ISBN: 0-7643-1919-1

Published by Schiffer Publishing Ltd.
4880 Lower Valley Road
Atglen, PA 19310
Phone: (610) 593-1777
FAX: (610) 593-2002
E-mail: Info@schifferbooks.com.
Visit our web site at: www.schifferbooks.com
Please write for a free catalog.
This book may be purchased from the publisher.
Please include $3.95 postage.
Try your bookstore first.

In Europe, Schiffer books are distributed by:
Bushwood Books
6 Marksbury Avenue
Kew Gardens
Surrey TW9 4JF
England
Phone: 44 (0) 20 8392-8585
FAX: 44 (0) 20 8392-9876
E-mail: info@bushwoodbooks.co.uk.
Free postage in the UK. Europe: air mail at cost.
Try your bookstore first.

CONTENTS

FOREWORD

This work, *U. S. Marine Corps Unit Insignia in the Republic of Vietnam 1961-1975*, is a significant contribution to the record of the Marine Corps' participation in the Vietnam War by chronicling the distinctive unit insignia, down to the battalion and squadron level, in support of our nation's commitment to a democratic way of life for the people of South Vietnam.

Unit insignia have long been of interest to military historian, Collectors, Veterans and families of those who have served with pride in our Nation's armed forces. Unfortunately, in the case of the United States Marine Corps, there is very little in print that identifies these insignia for the units that served so proudly in the Republic of Vietnam from 1961-1975. Fortunately, the author, Professor Eugene (Gene) Wilson, has rectified this void in our proud history.

A veteran of the war in Vietnam, Gene has been putting together his collection of over 350 Marine Corps unit insignia for more than 30 years. This collection of both official and unofficial unit insignia is clearly "one of a kind." Color scans of these insignia are in constant demand by historians, collectors, former Marines, and Marine veterans organizations. Now, with the publication of this authoritative, artfully illustrated book, this prize collection is available for all to view. Such a book is long overdue. For me, the book provides a reminder of my proud service. It also provides me with an opportunity to share with my family, friends, and fellow veterans the official and sometimes unofficial insignia of the units in which I proudly served.

This Marine is to be commended for his dauntless efforts to bring together this collection and to share it with us.

George R. (Ron) Christmas, USMC (Retired)
Lieutenant General, U.S. Marine Corps (Ret.)
President Marine Corps Heritage Foundation

INTRODUCTION

The use of distinctive unit insignia for the United States Marine Corps originated in France during World War I (1918). The first units within the Marine Corps to display individual unit shoulder sleeve insignia on their uniforms were the 5th and 6th Marine Regiments and the First Aviation Force, respectively. The crudely made cloth shoulder sleeve insignia (pictured on page 138) were worn by U. S. Marines to exhibit their *esprit de corps* while serving along side U.S. Army units as part of the American Expeditionary Force in France.

The practice of Marines wearing individual distinctive cloth unit insignia became official and was adopted Marine Corps-wide following World War I. This practice continued through World War II, culminating in some 45 shoulder sleeve insignia. The most notable in design was the Marine Raider Battalion Patch, with a skull within the slats of the Southern Cross constellation on a field of blue (pictured on page 139).

In 1947 the practice of Marine ground forces wearing individual unit insignia was abolished on the basis of "one corps - one insignia: the eagle, globe, and anchor." The only exception to the Commandant of the Marine Corps' instruction was Marines assigned to the Marine Aircraft Wing, who were authorized to wear unit insignia on flight clothing.

The wearing of individual unit insignia on a military uniform is a source of pride that builds morale among the members of that unit, and whether authorized or unauthorized, the practice exists. This time honored tradition of maintaining a distinctive unit insignia continues to be practiced to this day—the most notably individual unit insignia being that of the 1st Marine Reconnaissance Battalion (pictured on page 33); similar to its predecessor, the World War II era Randier Battalion, with skull and cross bones atop the Southern Cross constellation on a field of blue. While not authorized on the dress uniform and very seldom found on field uniforms for obvious operational considerations, the custom and tradition of distinctive unit insignia was very prevalent during the Vietnam war.

In Vietnam, Marines from units such as the Combined Action Program—who were involved in a grass-roots security operation and were assigned to rural areas to assist local militia in defense of a village—wore a small badge or pocket hanger type insignia. The Marines' Dog Handlers, serving in War Dog Platoons, also wore thin metal badges—commonly referred to as "Beer Cans"—on their jungle fatigue uniform to emphasize their respective specialty as a particular type of dog handler.

Given the length of the Marine Corps' fifteen year involvement in Southeast Asia many other examples of insignia can be found, in addition to locally procured embroidered cloth patches, such as End of Tour service plaques, Zippo cigarette lighters bearing a metal crest of the unit, coffee mugs adorned with hand painted unit insignia, and even "military payment certificate" money clips. The product of this practice of procuring items bearing a unit's insignia from a local vendor is commonly referred to as an "in-country" or theater made piece.

The patch designs, especially for the Marine ground forces included in this work, are not intended to be a complete or definitive representation of the respective unit's entire period of service in Vietnam. It was the author's goal to display at least one example of every Marine Corps unit's distinctive insignia with service in Vietnam down to at least the Battalion and Squadron levels, respectively.

It cannot be emphasized enough that this book is a compilation of not only the author's, but also quite a number of other former Marines and collectors that assisted in the chronicling of this period of Marine Corps history that has been otherwise overlooked.

This work is offered for its historical contribution by the author as a private citizen. The author does not attempt to trace military lineage or unit heraldry. Neither the United States Marine Corps nor any other component of the Department of Defense has approved, endorsed, or authorized this work.

III MAF CHRONOLOGY

The use of Distinctive Unit Insignia for the United States Marine Corps had it origin in France during World War I (1918). The first units within the Marine Corps to display individual unit shoulder sleeve insignia on their uniforms were the 5th and 6th Marine Regiments and the First Aviation Force, respectively. The crudely made cloth shoulder sleeve insignia, pictured on page 112, were worn by U. S. Marines to exhibit their *esprit de corps* while serving along side U. S. Army units as part of the American Expeditionary Force in France.

The practice of Marines wearing individual distinctive cloth unit insignia became official and adopted Marine Corps-wide following World War I. This practice continued through World War II culminating in some forty-five shoulder sleeve insignia. The most notable in design was the Marine Raider Battalion Patch with a skull within the stars of the Southern Cross constellation on a field of blue pictured on page 112.

In 1947, the practice of Marine ground forces wearing individual unit insignia was abolished on the basis of "one corps - one insignia: the eagle, globe and anchor". The only exception to the Commandant of the Marine Corps' instruction was Marines assigned to the Marine Aircraft Wing were authorized to wear unit insignia on flight clothing.

The wearing of individual unit insignia on a military uniform is a source of pride that builds moral among the members of that unit, whether authorized or unauthorized, the practice exists. This time honored tradition of maintaining a distinctive unit insignia is continued to be practice to this day. The most notably individual unit insignia being that of the 1st Marine Reconnaissance Battalion, pictured on page 25, like its predecessor the World War II era Randier Battalion with skull and cross bones atop the Southern Cross constellation on a field of blue. While not authorized on the dress uniform and very seldom found on field uniforms for the oblivious operational consideration, the custom and tradition of distinctive unit insignia was very prevalent during the Vietnam war.

In Vietnam, Marines from units such as the Combined Action Program involved in a grass-roots security operation were assigned to the rural areas to assist local militia in defense of a village wore a small badge or pocket hanger type insignia. The Marines Dog Handlers serving in War Dog Platoons also wore thin metal badges, which is commonly referred to as a "Beer Can" on their jungle fatigue uniform to emphasis their respective specialty as a particular type of Dog handler.

Given the length of the Marine Corps' fifteen year involvement in Southeast Asia many other examples of insignia can be found in addition to locally procured embroidered cloth patches such as, End of Tour service plaques, Zippo cigarette lighters bearing a metal crest of the unit, coffee mugs adorned with hand painted unit insignia and even money (MPC) clips. The product of this practice of procuring items bearing a unit's insignia from a local vendor is commonly referred to as a "in-country" or theater made piece.

The patch designs, especially for the Marine ground forces included in this work are not intended to be a complete or definitive representation of the respective unit's entire period of service in Vietnam. It was the author's goal to display at least one example of every Marine Corps unit's distinctive insignia with service in Vietnam down to at least the Battalion and Squadron levels respectively.

It cannot be emphasized enough that this book is a compilation of not only the authors, but also quite a number of other former Marines and collectors that assisted in the chronicling this period of Marine Corps history that has been otherwise overlooked.

This work is offered for its historical contribution by the author as a private citizen. The author does not attempt to trace military lineage or unit heraldry. Neither the United States Marine Corps nor any other component of the Department of Defense has approved, endorsed or authorized this work.

1

U.S. Marine Corps Command Elements

Defense Dept. photo (Marine Corps) 3rd MarDiv, *Da Nang*, Vietnam 12Apr65; "Marines march up the beach after making an amphibious landing at *Da Nang*, RVN". (Photo by Sgt. BATCHELOR)

U. S. Marine Corps Air and Ground Team Vietnam Insignia

U.S. Marine Corps Advisors
Mar 1962 - Mar 1973
NUC 10 May 65-30 Jun 69, 1 Jul 69-30 Jun 70,
1 Jul 70-31 Dec 71

Task Element, (79.3.3.6)
Apr 1962 - Dec 1964
Operation "Shu Fly" *Soc Trang*, RVN

Marine Unit Vietnam, (TU 79.3.5)
Jan 1965 - Mar 1965
Unofficial Beret worn by members of HMM-163
Commanded by Colonel John H. King Jr. USMC

9th Marine Expeditionary Brigade
Mar 1965 - 6 May 1965

III Marine Amphibious Brigade
Apr 1965 - May 1965; Apr 1971 - Jun 1971
MUC 14-27Jun71

9th Marine Amphibious Brigade
Mar 1965 - May 1965; Apr 1972 - Jul 1972

III Marine Expeditionary Force Shoulder Brassard
3 May 1965 - 7 May 1965 Redesignated as III MAF

III Marine Amphibious Force
7 May 1965 - 14 Apr 1971
NUC 6May65-30Jun68; 1Jul68-14Apr71

Third Marine Division
8Mar1965 - 30Nov1969; Mar - May 1975
PUC 8Mar65-15Sep67; MUC 1Jan-30Sep68

First Marine Division
1 Jul 1965 - Apr 1971
PUC 29Mar66-15Sep67, 1Sep67-31Oct68

Fifth Marine Division Components serving in Republic of Vietnam
RLT -26; RLT -27; including 13th Marine Regt Battalions
Jun 1966 - Nov 1971 (inclusive dates)

2

1st, 5th, and 7th Marine Regiments Infantry

DEFENSE DEPT. PHOTO (MARINE CORPS); 1st MarDiv, Vietnam 25Nov67; (Photographer: Sgt G. O. SULLIVAN, Jr.)
"Troops from 1st Battalion, 1st Marine Regiment working on Combat Operations Center Bunker at *Con Thien*, RVN".

1st Marine Regiment
Jan 1966 - May 1971
PUC 31Jan-2Mar68, 20Nov-9Dec68

1st Bn 1st Marine Regt
Aug 1965 - May 1971
PUC 29Aug65-9Oct66; MUC 14Apr-1May71

Above: **2nd Bn 1st Marine Regt**
Nov 1965 - May 1971
PUC 10Dec65-9Oct66; MUC 14Apr-1Jun71

Right:
3rd Bn 1st Marine Regt
Jan 1966 - May 1971
PUC 29Jun-29Mar66; NUC 23Jan-16Apr68, MUC 3Apr-12Apr69

Defense Dept. Photo (Marine Corps); 1stMAW, Vietnam 21Sep66; (Photographer: Cpl. EALSTEAD)
"LONELY VIGILANCE - a Marine sentinel's reflection shows in the water behind him as he searches the surrounding rice paddies for any sign of the *Viet Cong*".

5th Marine Regiment
May 1966 - Apr 1971
PUC 25Apr-5Jun67;MUC 23Jul-23Oct68

1st Bn, 5th Marine Regt
May 1966 - Apr 1971
PUC 14Aug65-29Mar66; NUC 3Mar70-24Mar71;
MUC 7-12Jun69, 2Aug-22Sep68

2nd Bn, 5th Marine
Apr 1966 - Mar 1971
PUC 6Jul65-29Mar65,14Sep67-3May68; MUC 9-11May69

Regt 3rd Bn, 5th Marine Regt
May 1966 - Mar 1971
PUC 1Sep65-29Mar66; MUC 30Jan-15Feb68

DEFENSE DEPT. PHOTO (MARINE CORPS); III MAF. Vietnam 2Nov66; (Photographer LCpl ALEJOS)
"Corporal W. A. RICE (San Francisco, Calif), who has been attached to H&S Company, 2nd Battalion, 7th Regiment, as a cook, serves rice to the people of *Phu Le* Hamlet, 15 miles south of *Chu Lai*, Vietnam, during a country fair Operation."

7th Marine Regiment
Aug 1965 - Sep 1970
MUC 4May-6Jul68

1st Bn, 7th Marine Regt
Aug 1965 - Sep 1970
PUC 14Aug65-19Mar66; MUC 24Oct-8Dec69, 21Apr-2May69

2d Bn, 7th Marine Regt
Aug 1965 - Oct 1970
PUC 6Jul65-20Mar66; NUC 8-20Dec65, 7-26Dec68

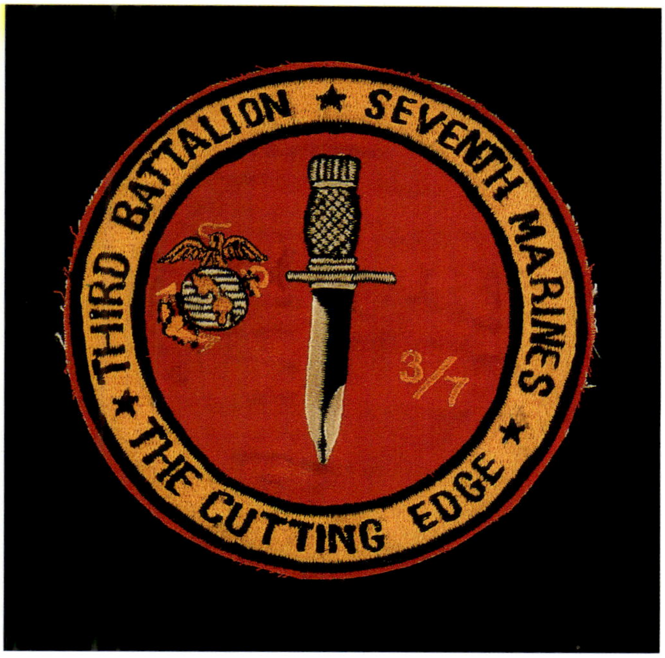

3d Bn, 7th Marine Regt
Sep 1965 - Oct 1970
PUC 1Sep65-29Mar66; MUC 23-27Feb69, 29Mar-29May69

3

3rd, 4th, and 9th Marine Regiments Infantry

DEFENSE DEPT. PHOTO (MARINE CORPS) III MAF, Vietnam 25Nov66;
"Marines pass Church ruins in *Quang Tri* Province. RVN". (Photographer: SSgt R. E.. WILSON)

3rd Marine Regiment
Mar 1965 - Sep 1969

st Bn, 3rd Marine Regt
Mar 1965 - Oct 1969
PUC 6Mar-11Aug65; MUC 4-8Jul68

2nd Bn, 3rd Marine Regiment
Apr 1965 - Nov 1969
PUC 10Apr-18Nov65; MUC 1Jan68-31May68

Regt 3rd Bn, 3rd Marine Regt
May 1965 - Oct 1969
PUC 13May65-30Apr66; NUC 30Apr-16May68; MUC 1May- 15Sep68

DEFENSE DEPT. PHOTO (MARINE CORPS) 3rdMarDiv, Vietnam 30Sep66;
"IN ACTION –Lance Corporal Charles M. HILL (Oseattle, Wyo), assistant gunner, and Sergeant Lee F. JANKES (Montgomery, Ala.), gunner, are shown firing on North Vietnamese troops on Hill *Nui-Cray-Tre* with their M60 machine gun. Both men are with the 3rd Battalion, 4th Marine Regiment, fighting near the demilitarized zone". (Photographer: PFC E. COLE)

4th Marine Regiment
Apr 1965 - Nov 1969

1st Bn, 4th Marine Regt
May 1965 - Nov 1969
PUC 7May65-15Dec66; NUC 29Nov-26Dec67

2d Bn, 4th Marine Regt
May 1965 - Nov 1969
PUC 7May65-27Oct66; NUC 5Mar-31May68

3rd Bn, 4th Marine Regt
Apr 1965 - Oct 1969
PUC 14Apr-23Dec65; MUC 13-31Jan68

DEFENSE DEPT. PHOTO (MARINE CORPS) 3rd MarDiv, Vietnam 1Oct65;
"Sergeant W. R. MELTON (Gridley Calif), Squad leader of 1st Squad, 2nd Platoon, Company "D", 1st Battalion, 9th Marines gather bodies of *Viet Cong* killed by the patrol during Operation "Golden Fleece" *Quang Nam* Province, RVN." (Photographer: Sgt. GORAC)

9th Marine Regiment
Mar 1965 - Aug 1969
Army PUC 23Jan-19Mar69; NUC 27Aug-8Oct68;
MUC 29Nov67-12Jan68, 24Oct68-19Jan69

st Bn, 9th Marine Regt
Jun 1965 - Aug 1969
PUC 17Jun65-19Sep66, 9Dec66-14Jan67,
Feb-15Sep67, 23Jan-31Mar68

2nd Bn,
9th Marine Regt
Jul 1965 - Aug 1969
PUC 6 Jul 65 - Sep 67
MUC 14-28 Sep 67

3rd Bn, 9th Marine Regt
Mar 1965 - Aug 1969
PUC 9Mar-12Jun65, 15Aug65-7Jan67; 1Mar-15Sep67;
MUC 17Jun-6Jul68, 7-12Jul68

4

26th and 27th Marine Regiments

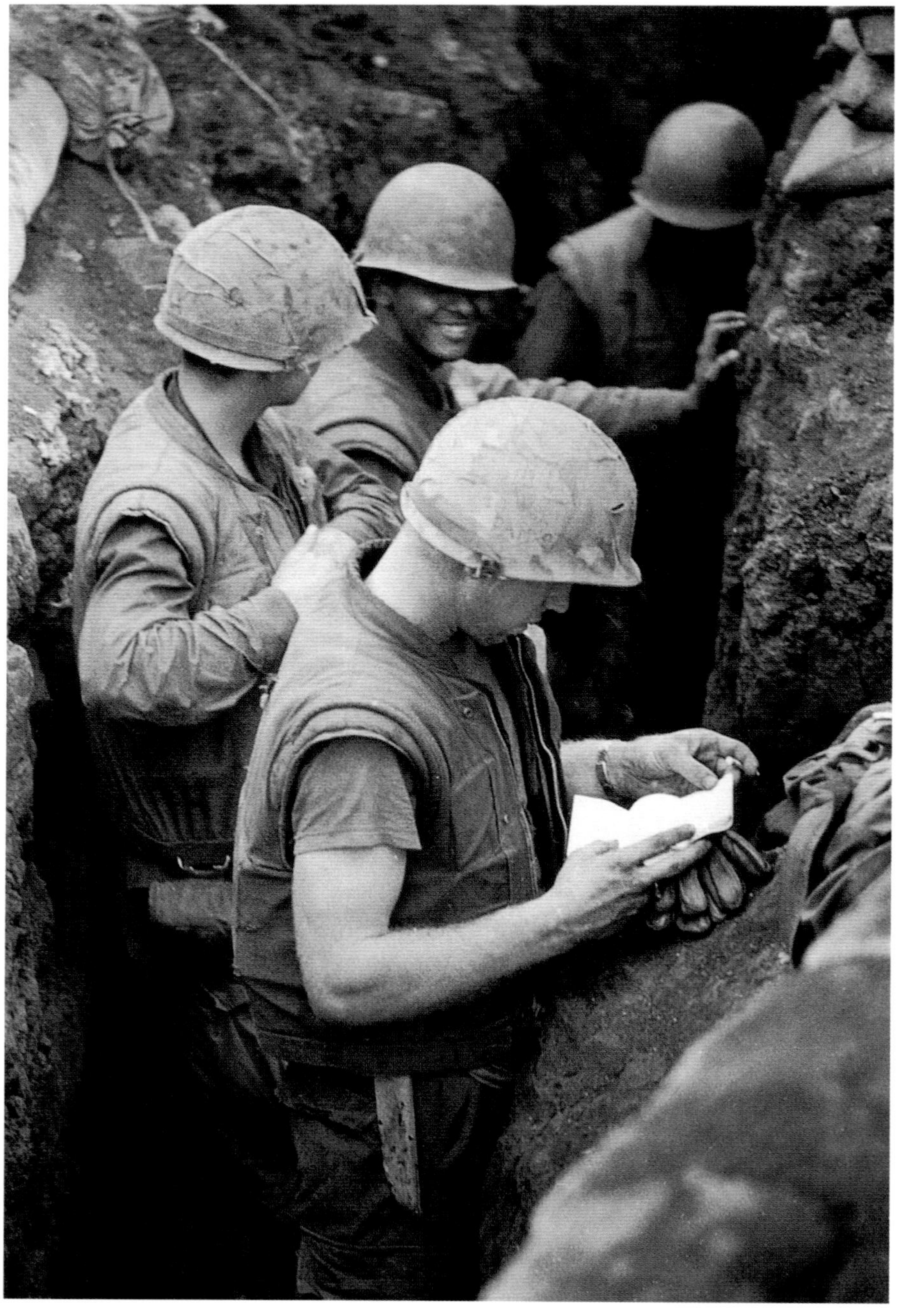

DEFENSE DEPT. PHOTO (MARINE CORPS) III MAF, Vietnam 4Mar68; (Photographer Cpl HALE) "Marines of "B" Co., Third Reconnaissance Battalion, Twenty-sixth Marines take a break digging trench to read their mail."

26th Marine Regiment
Aug 1966 - Mar 1970
PUC 20Jan-1Apr68

1st Bn, 26th Marine Regt
Sep 1966 - Mar 1970
PUC 2Aug-27Sep66, 29Sep66-15Sep67;
MUC 6Jun-16Jul68

2d Bn, 26th Marine Regt
Aug 1966 - Mar 1970
PUC 26Aug66-15Sep67, 20Jan31-Mar68; MUC 27Aug-5Oct68

3rd Bn, 26th Marine Regt
Aug 1966 - Mar 1970
PUC 5Oct-2Dec66, 5Dec66-15Sep67

DEFENSE DEPT. PHOTO (MARINE CORPS) 1stMarDiv, Vietnam 1966;
"A heavily laden Marine Rifleman steps across a hole in a rice paddy dike near *An Hoa*, Vietnam."

27th Marine Regiment
Feb 1968 - Sep 1968
PUC 1Feb-16May68, 29-31May68

1st Bn, 27th Marines Regiment
Feb 1968 - Sep 1968

2nd Bn, 27th Marine Regt
Feb 1968 - Sep 1968

3rd Bn, 27th Marine Regt
Feb 1968 - Sep 1968
PUC 17-28May68

5

Combined Action Force

The Combined Action Program's basic working unit was the Combined Action Platoon, consisting of a 13-man Marine rifle squad and a Navy corspman integrated with a platoon of local troops (Popular Forces). Its mission was to help the Vietnamese pacify and protect their own village or hamlet. The concept was based on the belief of helping the Vietnamese help themselves.

DEFENSE DEPT. PHOTO (MARINE CORPS) 3rd MarDiv Vietnam 24Dec67;
"Combined Action Platoon and villagers, Republic of Vietnam." (Photographer: Sgt BEHRENS)

1st Combined Action Group, *Chu Lai*
Oct 1967 - Sep 1970
PUC 1Jan-31Dec68; CAF NUC 1Aug65-31Dec67, 1Jan69-1Apr71
MUC 1Oct-31Dec67

2nd Combined Action Group, *Da Nang*
Oct 1967 - May 1971
PUC 17Jul-15Sep67; MUC 1Jun-31Dec68

3rd Combined Action Group, *Phu Bai*
Oct 1967 - Sep 1970
PUC 17Jul-15Sep67; MUC 1Oct-31Dec67

4th Combined Action Group, *Dong Ha*
Ju 1968 - Jul 1970
MUC 4Jan69-30Jul70

6

Reconnaissance

DEFENSE DEPT. PHOTO (MARINE CORPS) III MAF, Military Assistance Command, Vietnam "CONCENTRATION - Minutes before a Marine Aircraft Group-39 "Sea Knight" lands a 3rd Marine Division reconnaissance team in the rugged terrain west of Vandegrift Combat Base, one Marine's face is etched in concentration as he studies the area through which he'll be operating." (Photo by L/Cpl Jim De WITT)

1st Reconnaissance Battalion
Mar 1966 - Mar 1971
PUC 29Mar66-15Sep67; NUC 1Oct67-1Oct68, 1Jan70-31Dec70; MUC 1Jan-31Dec70

1st Force Reconnaissance Company
Oct 1965 - Apr 1971
PUC 9Mar65-27Apr66, 20Oct65-18Nov66; MJC 10Jan-7Sep68

3d Reconnaissance Battalion
May 1965 - Nov 1969
PUC 25Apr-15Sep67; NUC 22Sep65-15Mar66, 16Sep67-31Jul68; MUC 1Aug-30Sep68; Army Valorous Unit Award 7Dec69-15Sep70

3d Force Reconnaissance Company
Apr 1967 - Aug 1970
PUC 25Spr-15Sep67; MUC 15Sep67-31Jul67, 1Aug-30Sep68 Army Valorous Unit Award 7Dec69-15Feb70

7

11th, 12th, and 13th Marine Regiments Artillery

DEFENSE DEPT. PHOTO (MARINE CORPS) 3rdMarDiv, Vietnam 5Oct65;
"View of a 175mm self-propelled gun firing." (Photographer Sgt R. WOLTNER)

1st Bn, 11th Marine Regt
Jan 1966 - May 1971
PUC 16Sep-31Oct68,31Jan-2Mar69

2d Bn, 11th Marine Regt
Aug 1965 - Oct 1970
PUC 27Mar67-24Apr67

3d Bn, 11th Marine Regt
Aug 1965 - Oct 1970
PUC 16Sep67-2May68

4th Bn, 11th Marine Regt
Feb 1966 - Oct 1970
PUC 16Sep67-31Oct68

1st Bn, 12th Marine Regt
Aug 1965 - Sep 1969
PUC 10Apr65-15Sep67;
MUC 9Dec68-17Feb69

2d Bn, 12th Marine Regt
Jul 1965 - Aug 1969
PUC 13Jul65-15Sep67; MUC 29Nov67-13Jan68
Army PUC 22Jan-19Mar69

3d Bn, 12th Marine Regt
May 1970 - Nov 1969
PUC 7May65-15Sep67; MUC10Apr-16May68

4th Bn, 12th Marine Regt
Jul 1965 - Nov 1969
PUC 13Jul65-15Sep67; MUC 1Apr-15Aug68

1st Bn, 13th Marine Regt
Jul 1967 - Sep 1968
PUC 23Jul-15Sep67, 20Jan-31Mar68; MUC 1May-31Aug68

2nd Bn, 13th Marine Regt
Feb 1968 - Sep 1968
PUC 17fEB-31mAR68: MUC 10May68

3rd 8 inch Howitzer Battery Self Propelled
Mar 1966 - Jun 1971
PUC 20Nov-9Dec69

3rd 155mm Gun Battery
Aug 1965 - Sep 1970
NUC 7Dec68-9Mar69

8

1st Radio Battalion
5th and 7th Communication Bn

Photograph from the author's personal collection depicting a U.S. Marine Corps M151 Jeep belonging to the "Sunshine Electric Company" located at Marine Aircraft Group-*12* Marine Air Base, *Chu Lai*, RVN.

1st Radio Battalion, Detachment
Feb - Aug 1964
MUC 15Feb-15Aug64

1st Radio Battalion
Feb 1967 - Apr 1971
NUC Det "A" 15Feb-15Aug64, 31Oct68-31Jul69
MUC 1Aug69-9Mar70, 10Mar70-3Apr71

5th Communications Battalion
Nov 1965 - Oct 1970
PUC 30Jan-31Mar68; MUC 1Jan68-30Jun58,
MUC 6May65-22Jun71

7th Communications Battalion
Jul 1968 - Jun 1971
PUC 10Apr66-15Sep67; 16Sep-29Jan68
PUC 16Sep-29Jan68;MUC 29Jan-14Aug68

9

Engineer Battalions and Bridge Companies

DEFENSE DEPT. PHOTO (MARINE CORPS) III MAF, Vietnam 18Dec67; "Marines of "B" Company, 7th Engineers, rebuild Cooper bridge, named after a Marine Lance Corporal engineer who was killed while rebuilding the bridge an earlier time. The bridge has been blown and rebuilt two times before. It is about 10 miles south of *Da Nang* on Highway One. Construction is with mono tube piles, the only bridge built by Marines using this type piling."

1st Engineer Battalion
Jan 1966 - Mar 1971
PUC 29Mar66-15Sep67, 17Sep67-21Oct68; MUC 1Jun-31Jul70

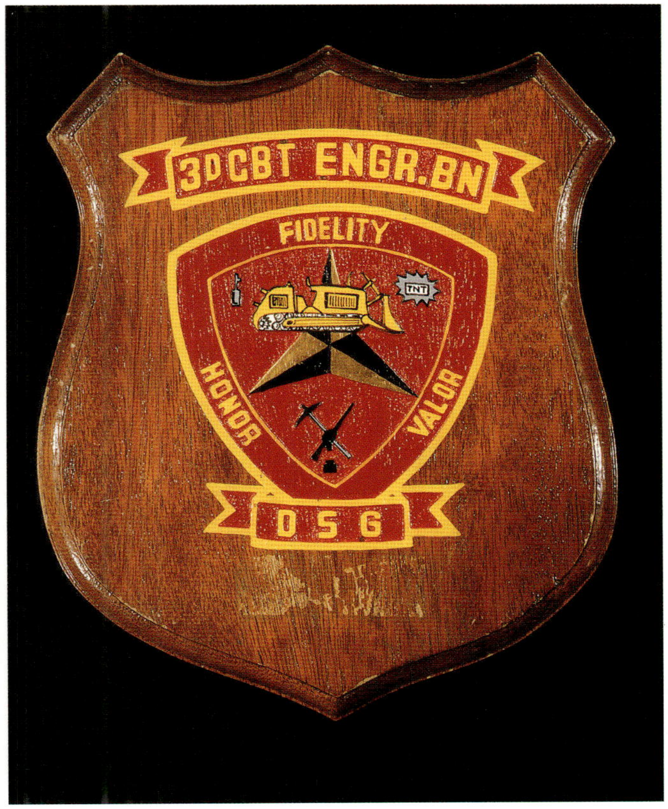

3d Engineer Battalion
Jul 1965 - Oct 1969
PUC 20Jan-31Mar68

7th Engineer Battalion
Aug 1965 - Dec 1970
PUC 1Apr66-15Sep67, 16Sep67-31Oct68
MUC 1Sep69-14May70

9th Engineer Battalion
May 1966 - Aug 1970
PUC 1Apr66-15Sep67, 21Apr67-30Apr68;
MUC 1Jul68-31May69; Army MUC 14Sep67-20Apr68

11th Engineer Battalion
Nov 1966 - Nov 1969
PUC 20Nov66-15Sep67; MUC 5Nov67-27Jan68

1st Bridge Company
Aug 1965 - Aug 1970
PUC 15Sep-31Dec67; MUC 1Jan-28Feb678

3d Bridge Company
Oct 1966 - Oct 1969
PUC 5-12Feb68; MUC 1Jan-28Feb68

DEFENSE DEPT. PHOTO (MARINE CORPS) III MAF Vietnam Apr68;
"U. S. Marines 11th Engineers work and move frame work of new bridge to replace bridge destroyed by North Vietnamese Army route #9 during Operation 'Pegasus'." (Photographer: SSgt J. A. RIED)

10

Motor Transport Battalions

1st Motor Transport Battalion
Apr 1966 - Apr 1971
PUC 29Mar66-15Sep67, 14Sep67-31Oct68

DEFENSE DEPT. PHOTO (MARINE CORPS) 3rd MarDiv, Vietnam, 28Nov67 (Photographer: LCpl BROWN)
"A truck convoy of the 1st Battalion, Third Marines, moves out of *Dong Ha* to *Con Thien* on Operation 'Newton'."

3d Motor Transport Battalion
Jun 1965 - Jul 1969
PUC 23Jun65-15Sep67

7th Motor Transport Battalion
May 1965 - Feb 1970
PUC 29Mar66-15Sep67, MUC 15Sep69-20Dec69

9th Motor Transport Battalion
Jul 1965 - Nov 1969
PUC14Jul65-15Sep67

11th Motor Transport Battalion
Dec 1966 - Apr 71
PUC 19Jun-15Sep67; MUC 16Sep67-31Dec68

11

1st and 3rd Tank Battalions & 1st and 3rd Anti-Tank Battalions

DEFENSE DEPT. PHOTO (MARINE CORPS) 3rdMarDiv Vietnam 29Jul67; (Photographer: LCpl L. P. BROWN)
Marines of 3rd Battalion, 4th Marine Regiment, provide security for one of the tanks of 3rd Tank Battalion within Demilitarized Zone on Operation "Kingfisher" that is taking place 2500 meters northwest of *Mui Con Thien*, RVN.

1st Tank Battalion
Mar 1966 - Mar 1970
PUC 29Mar-15Sep67; MUC 1Feb68-31Mar69

1st Anti Tank Battalion
Mar 1966 - Dec 1967
PUC 29Mar66-15Sep67, 16Apr66-21Dec67

3rd Tank Battalion
Jul 1965 - Oct 1969
PUC 16Jul65-15Sep67; MUC 28Jan-31May68

3rd Anti Tank Battalion
Ju 1965 - Dec 1967
PUC 12Jul65-15Sep67

DEFENSE DEPT. PHOTO (MARINE CORPS) 1stMarDiv, Vietnam 1967;
"A Marine Ontos (Anti-Tank Assault Vehicle) and Crew." (Photographer: SSgt UPTON)

3rd Anti-Tank Battalion

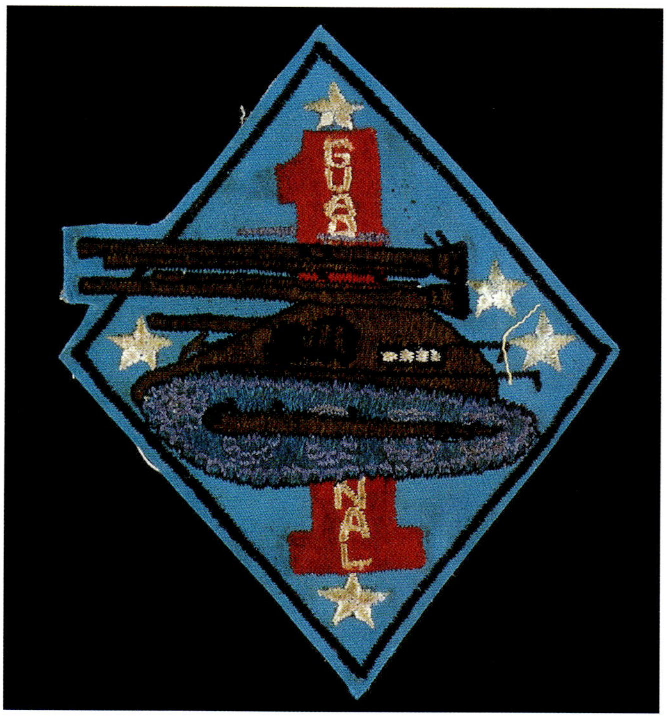

1st Anti-Tank Battalion

12

1st and 3rd Amphibious Tractor Battalions

DEFENSE DEPT. PHOTO (MARINE CORPS) 3rd MarDiv, Vietnam 9Sep72
"The surf is up and the first LVT (Landing Vehicle Tractor) of 1st Amphibious Tractor Battalion's 'B' Company splashes into the salty waters of the coast of *Quang Tri* area South Vietnam. From the LPD-10 USS Juneau during Operation *Lom Son*-72." (Photographer: CWO CONNOLLY)

1st Amphibian Tractor Bn
Jul 1965 - Jul 1969
PUC 1Jun-31Oct69; MUC 5Nov67-27Jan68, 26Aug-9Dec68

3d Amphibian Tractor Bn
Mar 1966 - Jan 1970
PUC 29Mar66-15Sep67; MUC 16Sep67-1Sep68

13

1st Air-Naval Gun Liaison Company & Aerial Observation Sections

Defense Dept. Photo (Marine Corps) 1st Mar Div, Vietnam May70; (Photographer: Sgt R. W. NELSON)
"After 8"gun turret turned to port side, one of the three 8" barrels fires over port side."

1st Air-Naval Gunfire Liaison Co.
unauthorized Beret Flash

SubUnit One 1st ANGLICO
April 1965 - January 1973
PUC 16Mar66-15Sep67, NUC 14-30Apr71; MUC 18Feb68-31Jul69, 1Apr72-10Sep72

1st Marine Div Observer Section
Mar 1966 - Apr 1971
PUC 25Apr-5un67; MUC 20Nov68-13Aug69

3rd Marine Div Observer Unit
Apr 65 - Nov 1969
MUC 14Apr-31Mar68, 17Oct68-30Jun69, 10Apr-14May68

14

Force Logistic Command
1st and 3rd Force Service Regiments

DEFENSE DEPT. PHOTO (MARINE CORPS), III MAF, Vietnam 14Ju 67; (Photographer: SSgt GATERMAN)
"Aerial oblique of Front View of Force Logistics Command Headquarters building, *Da Nang*, RVN."

Force Logistic Command
Mar 1966 - Jul 1971
NUC 12Mar65-15Mar67, 16Mar67-31May68,
1Jun68-31Mar69, MUC 1Jul70-26Jun71

Force Logistic Support Group-B
Mar 1966 - Sep 1970

1st Force Service Regiment
Feb 1967 - Apr 1971
NUC 18-23Aug65

3d Force Service Regiment
Mar 1965 - Oct1968
MUC 12May65-30Sep68

15

1st and 3rd Shore Party Battalions

DEFENSE DEPT. PHOTO (MARINE CORPS) 3rd MarDiv, *Da Nang* Vietnam 3Aug65
"U. S. Marines landing at *Da Nang*. Republic of Vietnam."

1st Shore Party Battalion
Apr 1965 - Nov 1969
PUC29Mar66-15Sep67; Co "A" MUC 3May-7Jul68

3d Shore Party Battalion
Apr 1965 - Nov 1969
MUC 1Jan-31Jul68

16

1st and 3rd Medical Battalions
1st Hospital Company
1st, 3rd, and 11th Dental Companies

DEFENSE DEPT. PHOTO (MARINE CORPS) 3rd MarDiv *Da Nang*, S. Vietnam 26Mar65;
"Tent used for laboratory work; stretcher used for shock patients at the Untied States Naval Hospital, *Da Nang*." (Photographer: SSgt. H. C. BATCHELOR)

1st Medical Battalion
Mar 1966 - Apr 1970
PUC 15Sep67-21Oct68; ; MUC 3Apr68-15May69

1st Hospital Company
Mar 1966 - Feb 1970
PUC 29Mar66-15Sep67

1st Dental Company
Mar 1966 - Feb 1970
PUC 15Sep67-31Oct68; MUC 23Mar68-31Mar69, 16May69-26Sep70

11th Dental Company
Mar 1966- Jun 1971
PUC 20Mar66-15Sep67; NUC 1Sep67-1Sep68; MUC 14Apr-27Jun71

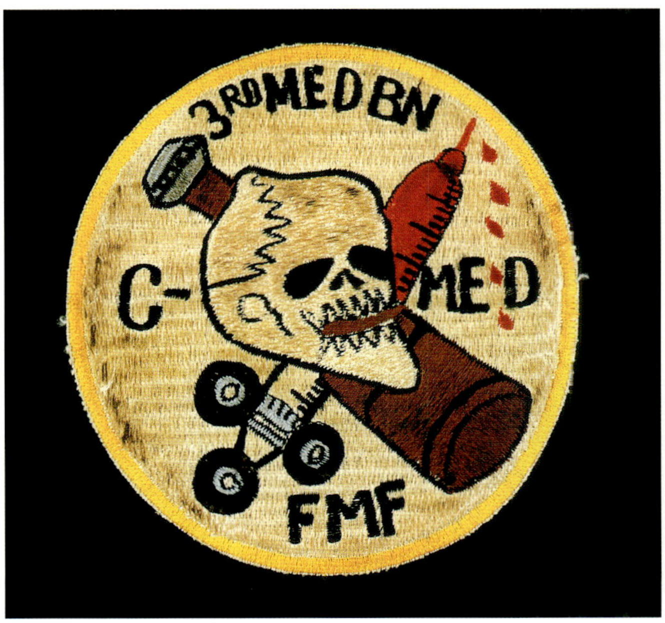

3rd Medical Battalion
Jun 1965 - Nov 1969
NUC 7Jul65-20Feb66, 1Jan-31Mar68

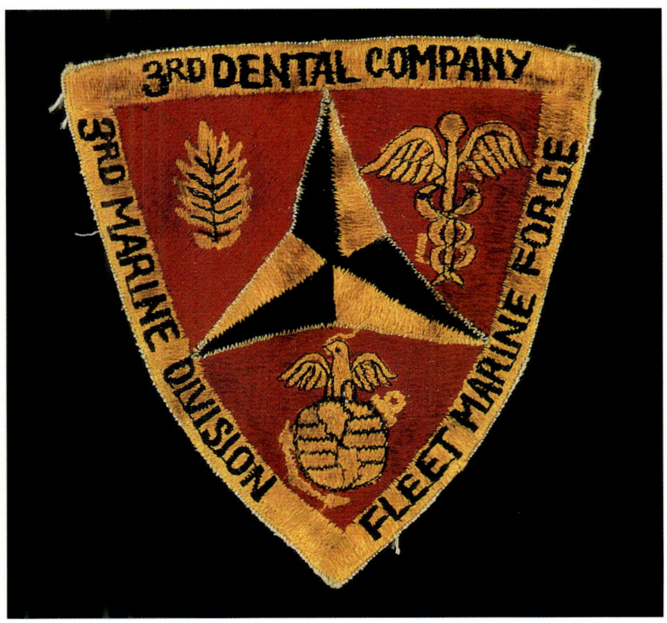

3d Dental Company
Jun 1965 - Nov 1969
PUC 20Jan-31Mar68; MUC 26Aug-9Dec69

17

1st and 3rd Military Police Battalions

DEFENSE DEPT. PHOTO (MARINE CORPS) 1st MarDiv, Vietnam, 1967; (Photographer Ssgt UPTON)
"Patrol truck driver, Lance Corporal Gilbert J. SHAW, stands by in his truck in case his patrol is needed."

1st Military Police Battalion
May 1966 - Jun 1971
PUC 12Jan66-15Sep67; MUC 1Jun68-30Jun69

3d Military Police Battalion
May 967 - Aug 1970
MUC 31May67-31May68, 21May67-21May68
5Apr67-31May68, 1Jul70-14Apr71 1Aug68-30Apr69, 1Jul-24Aug70

18

Scout, Sentry, & Mine and Booby Trap Detection Dogs

DEFENSE DEPT. PHOTO (MARINE CORPS) FLC Vietnam 2Dec69; (Photographer: Cpl Nick MYERS)
TWO MARINE SENTRIES - Cpl John HACKETT (23 Avlets Ave., San Francisco, Calif.) and Sarge (formerly owned by William JAMES, 15 Fortlace Dr., East Falmouth, Mass.) look down on the sunset over *Da Nang*, in the Republic of Vietnam. Sarge and Hackett are stationed atop Monkey Mountain near *Da Nang*, where they guard the perimeter of Marine Aircraft Control Squadron 4. They are attached to the 3rd Military Police Battalion, Force Logistic Command *Da Nang*, RVN.

1st & 2nd Scout Dog Platoon
Aug 1965 - Apr 1971
PUC 20Nov-9Dec68; MUC29Mar-29May69
Army PUC 22Jan-19Mar69

1st & 2nd Sentry Dog Platoon
Mar 1966 - Apr 1971
MUC 15Sep67-1Sep68, 29Mar-29May69

1st Platoon, Mine & Booby Trap Detection Dogs
1970 - Apr 1971
MUC 3May70-24Mar71

1st Platoon Mine & Booby Trap Detection Dogs
1970 - Apr 1971

19

Marine Security Guard Detachment
United States Embassy
Saigon, Republic of Vietnam

UNITED STATES ARMY PHOTOGRAPHIC AGENCY, WASH DC, *Saigon* RVN 15Feb68;
"*VIET CONG* ATTACK AMERICAN EMBASSY— Military Police watch for enemy activity inside the grounds of the Embassy." (Photographer: U.S. Army SP5 Edgar PRICE)

Marine Security Guard
U.S. Embassy, Saigon RVN
Evacuated 29Apr1975

Company "E", MSG Battalion
NUC 29-30Apr75; MUC 1Feb69-31Dec70

20

1st Marine Aircraft Wing Command Elements

1st Marine Aircraft Wing Vietnam - Unofficial Dragon Patch

DEFENSE DEPT. PHOTO (MARINE CORPS) 1st MAW, Vietnam 25Nov70; "First Marine Aircraft Wing Headquarters Compound." (Photographer: Capt C.H. ARMSTRONG)

1st Marine Aircraft Wing
May 1965 - Apr 1971
PUC 11May65-15Sep67

1st Marine Aircraft Wing

1st Marine Air Wing Operations

1st Marine Aircraft Wing
"Sports Program"

Marine Wing Headquarters Group-1
May 1965 - Apr 1971
PUC 20Jun65-15Sep57; MUC 1Sep67-1Sep68

Headquarters & Headquarters Squadron-1
May 1965 - May 1971
PUC 10Jun65-15Sep67; MUC 1Sep67-1Sep68

Marine Air Control Group-18
Oct 1967 - Apr 1971
PUC 1-15Sep67; NUC 1Oct67-30Apr68

Headquarters & Headquarters Squadron-18
Oct 1967 - Apr 1971
PUC 1-15Sep67; MUC 1Oct67-30Apr68

Marine Wing Facilities Squadron-1
1967 - 1971
MUC 1Sep67-1Sep68

Marine Wing Communications Squadron-1
1967 - 1971
PUC 1-15Sep67; MUC 1 Sep67-1Sep68

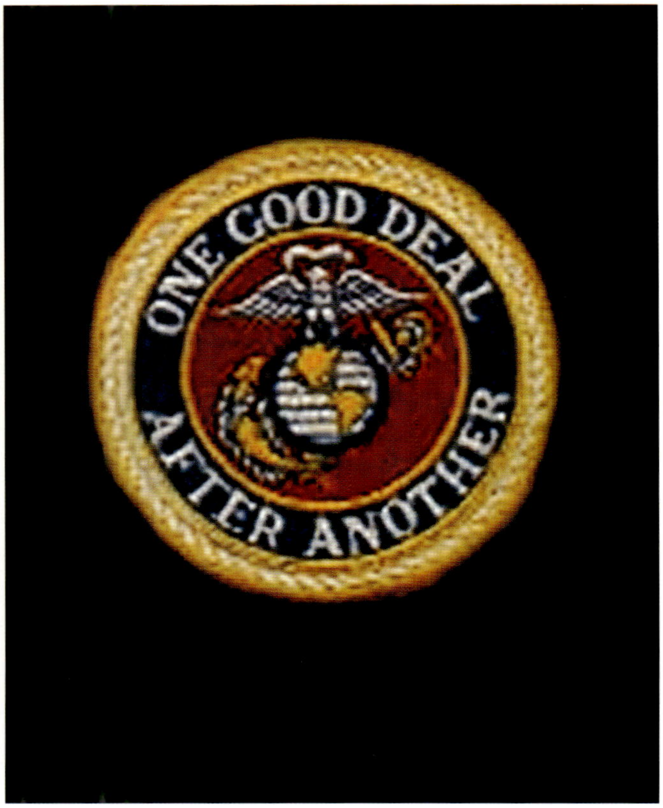

21

MASS
Marine Aircraft Support Squadrons

Marine Air Support Squadron-2
Apr 1965 - 1971
PUC 14Apr65-15Sep67; MUC 1Oct67-30Apr68

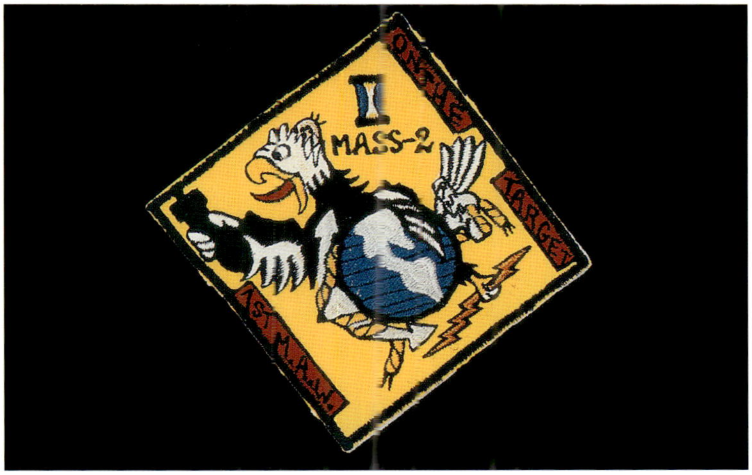

Marine Air Support Squadron-2

Marine Air Support Squadron-3
1966 - 1971
PUC 8Nov66-15Sep67; MUC 1May68-20May71

22

MACS
Marine Aircraft Control Squadrons

Marine Air Control Squadron-4
Jun 1967 - Apr 1971

Marine Air Control Squadron-7
1965 - 1967
PUC 11Aug65-15Sep67

Marine Air Control Squadron-9
1965
PUC 11May-14Sep65

23

MATCU
Marine Air Traffic Control Units

Marine Air Traffic Control Unit-62
1966 -1971, Jun - Dec 1972 TF Delta
PUC 28NOv66-15Sep67; NUC 13Oct68-30Jun69
NUC 14Jun-31Dec72

Marine Air Traffic Control Unit-66
SU Provisional MAG-39
NUC 14Aug68-24Auf68, 25Aug-16Oct68

Marine Air Traffic Control Unit-67
1965 - 1970
PUC 15May65-15Sep67; NUC 1Apr68-15Sep69

Marine Air Traffic Control Unit-68
1965 - 1971
PUC 1Jul65-15Sep67; NUC 15Apr68-15Sep69

Marine Air Traffic Control Unit-70
1967 - 1968

24

Marine Aerial Refueling and Transport Squadrons Marine Composite Reconnaissance and Electronic Countermeasure Squadrons

VMGR-152
1963 - 1975 (KC-130 Hercules)
MUC 25Jan-13Feb70, 22Jun70-24May71

VMGR-352
Jun 1965 - Oct 1972
NUC 15Jul-4Aug66; SU 1 MUC 1Jan-30Sep68

VMCJ-1
Apr 1965 - Jul 1970 (EA-6B Prowler)
NUC 17Apr-1Nov65;MUC 16Sep-30Sep67, 11May-1Nov68

VMCJ-2
Apr 1972 - Feb 1973
aboard USS *Saratoga* (CVA-60)
MUC 19May72-9Jan73

25

MWSG-17
Marine Wing Support Group 17

Marine Wing Support Group-17
1965 - 1970
PUC 11Sep66-15Sep67; MUC 1968

Headquarters & Maintenance Squadron-17
1965 - 1970
PUC 21Mar66-15Sep67

Wing Equipment Repair Squadron-17
1965 - Aug 1970
PUC 31Jul66-15Sep67; MUC 1Jan-31Dec68

26

MAG-11
Marine Aircraft Group 11

DEFENSE DEPT. PHOTO (MARINE CORPS) 1stMAW, *Da Nang*, RVN
"Marine Aircraft Group-11 Base Chapel."

Marine Aircraft Group-11
Jul 1965 - Feb 1971
NUC 1Nov70-10Jun71

Headquarters & Maintenance Squadron-11
Apr 1965 - Feb 1971
PUC 7Jul65-15Sep67; MUC 1Jul68-31Jan69

Marine Air Base Squadron-11
Apr 1965 - Feb 1971
PUC 7Jul65-15Sep67; MUC1Jan-31Dec68, 1Jan-31Oct70

Marine Air Group-11 "Avionics"

Marine Air Group-11 "Think Tank"

VMFA-115
Oct 1965 - Aug 1973 (F-4B Phantom II)
PUC 11Oct65-12Jan66; NUC 21May-1Jun70

VMFA-122
Aug 1967 - Sep 1972
PUC 1Sep67; NUC 1Oct67-30Aug68

VMFA-122

VMFA-122

VMFA-212
Apr 1965; Apr - Jun 1972
MUC 1Apr-20Jun72

VMFA-314
1965- Sep 1970 (F4-B Phantom II)
PUC 13Jan-13Apr66; MUC 1Jan69-1May70

VMFA-314

VMFA-323
Dec 1965 - Mar 1969
PUC 1Dec65-20Feb66; NUC 26-30Apr65

VMFA-232
Mar 1968 - Sep 1969 (F-4 Phantom)
NUC 27Mar68-7Sep69

VMFA-334
Sep 1968 - Jul 1969 (F-4J Phantom)
MUC 29Feb-28Aug69, 10Aug-24Jun69

VMFA-513
Jun 1965 - Oct 1965
PUC 15Jun-15Oct65; NUC 18-23Aug65

VMFA-531
Apr 1965 - Jul 1965 (F-4 Phantom)
PUC 11May-15Jun65; NUC 10Apr-15Jun65

VMFA-542
Jul 1965 - Jan 1970 (F-4B Phantom)
PUC 10Jul-1Dec65; NUC 18-23Aug65; MUC 10May-31Dec68

VMF(AW)-232
Dec 1966 - Sep 1967 (F-8U Crusader)
PUC 5Nov66-15Sep67

VMF(AW)-212
Jun 1967 - Jan 1968 (F-8U Crusader)
PUC 15Nov66-15Sep67

VMF(AW)-235
1966, 1967 - 1968

VMF(AW)-312
Dec 1965 - Jan 1966
PUC 1Feb-15Nov66; MUC 1Oct67-10May68

VMA(AW)-225

VMA(AW)-225
Jan 1969 - May 1971 (A-6A Intruder)

27

MAG-12
Marine Aircraft Group 12

Photograph from author's personal collection of the Marine Aircraft Group-12 headquarter's signboard located at the *Marine*, Air Base *Chu Lai*, Republic of Vietnam.

Chu Lai Air Base, RVN
May 1965 - Oct 1970
May 1972 - Jan 1973

Marine Aircraft Group-12
PUC 14May65-15Sep67; NUC7May65-15Apr66,
NUC 17May72-21Dec72, 1Apr68-31Mar69

Headquarters & Maintenance Squadron-12
1965 - 1970, 1972 - 1973
PUC 25May65-15Sep67; MUC 15Sep67-31Mar68

Marine Air Base Squadron-12
1965 - 1970, 1972 - 1973
PUC 11May65-15Sep67; MUC 15Sep67-31Mar68

MAG-12 Intelligence

MABS-12, Utilities Section

MCAF, Chu Lai "Fire"

VMA-121
Aug 1966 - 1969 (A-4 Skyhawk)
PUC 10Nov66-3Jun67; NUC 15Sep67-31Mar68

VMA-211
Oct 1965 - May 1972 (A-4E Skyhawks)
PUC 11Oct65-13Jul66; MUC 1Apr68-31Mar69

VMA-214
Jun 1965 - Apr 1967 (A-4 Skyhawks)
PUC 13Jun65-15Feb66; MUC 7May-17Aug65

VMA-223
Dec 1965 - Feb 1970 (A-4B Skyhawk)
PUC 15Dec65-1Dec66; MUC 7May65-30Nov66

VMA-223

VMA-224
Oct 1965 - Oct 1966
PUC 1Oct65-30Apr66; NUC 7May65-15Apr66

VMFA-333
Jun 1972 - Mar 1973 USS *America* (CVA-66)
MUC 14Jul72-20Feb73

VMA(AW)-242
Nov 1966- Sep 1970 (A-6A Intruder)
PUC 15Nov66-15Sep67; NUC 11May68-1Feb69

VMA(AW)-533
Apr 1967 - Mar 1969
PJC 1Apr-15Sep67; MUC 15Sep67-31Mar69
MUC 14Sep67-10May68

28

MAG-13
Marine Aircraft Group 13

Defense Dept. Photo (Marine Corps) 1st MarDiv Vietnam Dec67
"Marine Aircraft Group-13 Hangers, *Chu Lai*, RVN."

Marine Aircraft Group-13
Oct 1966 - Oct 1970
PUC 1Oct66-15Sep67; NUC 15Sep67-30Apr68

Headquarters & Maintenance Squadron-13
1965 - Oct 1970
PUC 1Sep66-15Sep67; MUC 1May69-20May70

Marine Air Base Squadron-13
1965 - 1970
PUC 7Sep66-15Sep67; MUC 15Sep67-30Apr69

H&MS-13 "Flight Line"

MAG-13 "Medical"

VMA-225
May 1965 - Oct 1965
PUC 1Jun-5Oct65; NUC 7May-17Aug65; MUC 1Aug68-4Feb69

VMA-311
Apr 1965 - Jan 1973
PUC 1Jun-15Dec65; NUC 18-23Aug65

VMA-311

29

MAG-16
Marine Aircraft Group 16
Helicopters

DEFENSE DEPT. (MARINE CORPS) 1st MAW, Vietnam 12Nov66;
"FIRST IN...First Marine Division Marines run to set up secured positions as they deploy in a rice paddy 20 miles north of *Chu Lai*. Brought to the landing zone by CH-46 'Sea Knight' helicopters of the First Marine Aircraft Wing the First Division Marines participated in a search and clear operation against insurgent communist forces." (Photographer: Sgt B. C. HATHAWAY)

Marine Aircraft Group- 16, MMAF
Mar 1965 - May 1971
PUC 11May65-15Sep67; NUC 1Nov70-31May71

Headquarters & Maintenance Squadron-16
1965 - 1971
PUC 11May65-15Sep67; MUC 20Nov68-13Aug69

Marine Air Base Squadron-16
Mar 1965 - 1971
PUC 11May65-15Sep67; NUC 20Nov68-13Aug69

MAG-16 (-) Motor Transport Section

HML-167
Jun 1968 - Jun 1971
MUC 1Oct-31Dec69

HMM-161
May 1965 - Sep 1970
PUC 11May65-3Jan66; MUC 18-23Aug65

HMM-161

HMM-162
Jan 1963 - Jun 1963
PUC 11-15May65; NUC 13Jan62-6Jun62, 1Jul-7Oct64

HMM-162

HMM-165
Sep 1966 - Aug 1969
PUC 1Oct66-24Apr67; NUC 23Jan-14Apr68

HMM-165
Apr - May 1975
MUC Apr - May75

HMM-261
Jan 1963 - May 1966
PUC 23Jun65-27May66; MUC 4Sep65-14Aug66

HMM-265
May 1966 - Oct 1969 (CH-46A)
PUC 22May66-11Jul67, 24Aug-15Sep67

HMM-263
Aug 1965 - Apr 1971
PUC 10Oct65-22Mar66; NUC 19Jan-13Aug69

HMM-364
Feb 1964 - Mar 1971
PUC 31Aug65-10Apr66; NUC 4Sep65-24Aug66

HMM-364

HMM-365
May - Aug 1965
PUC 15May-2Aug65

HMH-361
Ju[illegible] 1969 - Feb 1970 (CH-53A Sea Stallion)

HMH-463
Jan 1967 - Jul 1973
PUC 9Jan-24Apr67; MUC 15Sep-31Oct67

HMH-463
Apr 1975
Operations "Frequent Wind" & "Eagle Pull"
NUC 29-30Apr75; MUC 12Apr75

30

MAG-36
Marine Aircraft Group 36
Helicopters

DEFENSE DEPT. PHOTO (MARINE CORPS) 1st MAW, Vietnam 24Jul66;
DEFENDERS - - PFC Harry L. DANIELSON (Wisconsin), phones the company command post while PFC Lawrence A. SCHINDLER (Pittsburg, Pa.) mans the M60 machine gun on the Marine Aircraft Group (MAG-36) perimeter. (Photographer: PFC Russell OWEN)

Marine Aircraft Group-36, Ky Ha AF
Sep 1965 - Oct 1969
PUC 11Aug65-15Sep67; NUC 4Sep65-14Aug66;

Headquarters & Maintenance Squadron - 36
Sep 1965 - Oct 1969
PUC31Aug65-15Sep67; MUC 31Jan-2Mar68

Marine Air Base Squadron - 36
Sep 1965 - Oct 1969
PUC 31Aug66-15Sep67; NUC 4Sep65-24Aug66

MAG-36 Group Supply

HML-367
Mar 69 - Jun 71 (UH-1E, AH-1G)
NUC 15Nov70-24May71; MUC1Mar-31Dec69

HML-367
Apr 1975
MUC 29-30Apr75

HMM-164
Jul 1966 - Oct 1969
PUC 5Mar66-3Apr67; MUC 31Jan-2Mar68
MUC 13May-23Jul72

HMM-164 (CH-46D)
Apr 1975 Operation "Frequent Wind"
"Lifted Last Americans out Marine Security Force"
Aboard USS *Okinawa* (LPH-3)

HMM-164

USMC-USN GUN CLUB

HMM-361
Oct 1963 - 1970
PUC 2Aug65-1Apr66; NUC 18-23Aug65

HMM-361

HMM-362 (reinf), Operation "SHU-FLY"
Apr 1962 - Aug 1962 (HUS-1/UH-34D)
"First Helicopter Crew to serve In-Country "

HMM-362
1965 - 1969
PUC 31Aug65-9Jan66; MUC 4Sep65-24Aug66

HMM-363
1965-1966
PUC 31Aug65-3Jul66; NUC 4Sep65-24Aug66

HMH-462 (CH-53A)
Aug 1968 - Apr 1971
NUC 29-30Apr75; MUC 1Sep68-Mar69

31

MAG-39 (Provisional) Marine Aircraft Group 39

DEFENSE DEPT. PHOTO (MARINE CORPS) III MAF, Military Assistance Command, Vietnam
ARTY SET UP - "A Sea Stallion of Marine Heavy helicopter Squadron 462 delivers a load of equipment at an artillery fire support base during a recent operation west of *Khe Sanh*, Vietnam. During the past three months, the HMH-462 heavy haulers carried nearly 18,000 tons of equipment, food and ammunition to outposts along the Demilitarized Zone and in elsewhere in the northern I Corps tactical area." (Photo by Sgt. C. E. HEARD)

Marine Aircraft Group-39 (Provisional) Quang Tri, AF
Apr 1968 - Jul 1969; Apr 1975
NUC 16Apr-16Oct, MUC 17Oct68-30Jun69

Sub Unit H&MS-39
Apr 1968 - Jul 1969
MUC 14Apr-14Oct68, 17Oct68-30Jun69

MAG-39, Security Element

HMM-163
Aug 1962 - Jul 1971
PUC 11May-10Oct65; MUC 18-22Aug65

HMM-262
Dec 1966 -May 1971
PUC 15Dec65-24Apr67, 6Jun-22Aug67, 25Apr-5Jun67

HMA-369
Jun 1972- Jan 1973
Aboard USS *Tripoli* (AH-1J Sea Cobra)
NUC 22Jun72-18Jan73; MUC 29Apr-30Apr75

HMA-369
Jun 1972 - Jan 1973
"Hunter Killer Operations"

HMA-369
Apr 1975 Aboard USS *Denver* (LPH-9)
Operation "Frequent Wind" MUC 29-30 Apr 75

32

Observation Squadrons - VMO

VMO-2 Marine Observation Squadron
Apr 1962 - Apr 1971 (O-1B, OV-10, UH-1E)
PUC 1965-1967; NUC 17Apr-1Nov65, 1Nov65-20Sep66

VMO-3
Dec 1966 - Feb 1969 (Redesignated HML-367)
PUC 10Dec65-24Apr67; MUC 29Jan-14Feb68

VMO-6
Aug 1965 - Oct 1969 (O1-E/UH-1E)
PUC 1Sep65-24Apr67, 6Jun-15Sep67, NUC 1Sep65-24Aug66

VMO-6 Ordnance Chu Lai, Republic of Vietnam

33

Tactical Air Controller - Airborne

Tactical Air Control, 0-1 Det
1966 - 1968 (O-1E Cessna C-170 "Birddog")

Tactical Air Control (A), 0-1 Charlie
1966 - 1968
MUC 1Apr-11Jul68

Klondike Playboy - TAC (A)
1966 - 1968 (UH-1E)

Playboy TAC (A)
1969 - 1970 (TA-4F)

34

Anti-Aircraft Missile Battalions

1st Light Anti-Aircraft Missile Battalion
Feb 1965 - 1969
PUC 11May65-15Sep67

1 st LAAM Battalion
Batteries "H&S, A, B"

2nd Light Anti-Aircraft Missile Battalion
Sep 1965 - Oct 1968
PUC 11Sep65-15Sep67

1st LAAM Bn Battery "C"

35

Marine Aircraft Group 15 (MCAS Rose Garden) Nam Phong, Thailand

DEFENSE DEPT. PHOTO (MARINE CORPS) FMF Pac *Nam Phong*, Thailand 11Jul72;
Aerial view of Tent City, the billeting area for Headquarters and Maintenance Squadron-15 and Marine Air Base Squadron-15 looking South. (Photographer: Sgt D. N. KOTALAS)

Rose Garden #1
Task Force Delta Nam Phong, Thailand
NUC 23May72-31Dec72; MUC 23May72-31Dec72

Rose Garden variation

Marine Aircraft Group-15
Jun - Dec 1972
MUC 21Jun-31Dec72

Headquarters & Maintenance Squadron-15
Jun - Dec 1972
MUC 21Jun-31Dec72

Marine Air Base Squadron-15
Jun - Sep 1972
MUC 21Jun-31Dec72

H&MS-15, Ordnance

MAG-15, Det "A"
Fleet Image Interpretation Unit

MAG-15 Communications

Rose Garden, Triple Squadron Insignia
"VMFA-115, VMFA-232, VMA(AW)-533" Jun - Dec 1972
(F-4B Phantom II)

VMFA-115

VMFA-232
Jun - Dec 1972 (F-4J Phantom II)
NUC 21Jun-31Dec72

VMFA-232

VMA(AW)-533
Jun - Dec 1972 (A-6A Intruder)
NUC 21Jun - 31Dec72

VMA(AW)-533 *"unauthorized"*

VMA(AW)-533

VMGR-152 Det. "D"
May 1972 - Oct 1972 (KC-130 Hercules)
NUC 20Jun-31Dec72

3rd Force Service Regiment
H&S Co. SU 1, Task Force Delta
NUC 21Jun-31Dec72, MUC 21Jun-31Dec72

MCAS Rose Garden

Turn Around Crew

MCAS, Nam Phong Security Element

Rose Garden Survivor

MCAS, Rose Garden Survivor

VMA(AW)-224
Dec 1971 - Jun 1972 (A6-A Intruder)
Aboard USS *Coral Sea* (CVA-43), NUC Dec71-Jun72

USS Coral Sea (CVA-43)
Nov 1971 - Jul 1972
6th Vietnam War Cruise

Official Navy Photograph, Naval Photographic Center, Naval Station ,Washington D.C. (1Feb62)
"AIR TO AIR A4D - A/C-A4-IN FLIGHT" (Marine Corps Attack Squadron VMA-242).

Official Navy Photograph, Naval Photographic Center, Naval Station ,Washington D.C. (19May70)
"Gulf of Tonkin, RVN.... The Attack Aircraft Carrier USS *Coral Sea* (CVA-43) underway."
(Photographer PH2 George W. ESTAVER)

36

Operation "End Sweep" Task Force 78

DEFENSE DEPT. PHOTO (MARINE CORPS), Vietnam Mar73, "Delegates look at CH53A Sea Stallion"
Operation ENDSWEEP was tasked with the clearance of US-laid sea mines from *Hiaphong* Harbor.

Operation End Sweep "TF 78"
12 Mar - 30 Jul 1973

Operation End Sweep "TF-78"

HML-167

HMM-164

HMM-165

HMH-463

HMH-463

HMH-463

37

Other U.S. Services U.S. Army, U.S. Air Force, and U.S. Navy Serving with the III MAF

U. S. ARMY PHOTOGRAPHIC AGENCY WASH DC; Vietnam 2Oct69;
U. S. Marines board a CH-47 "Chinook" helicopter during the joint Army, Marine Corps and ARVN Operation "Utah Mesa" in the *A Shaw* Valley, Republic of Vietnam. (Photographer: U.S. Army SP5 Ronald Bammeren)

U.S. and Allied Forces serving with the U.S. Marine Corps

Military Assistance Command Vietnam Studies & Observation Group

U.S. Army Headquarters, XXIV Corps

U.S. Army 101st Airborne Division (Airmobile)

U.S. Army 3d Brigade, 82nd Airborne Division

U.S. Army 1st Cavalry Division (Airmobile)

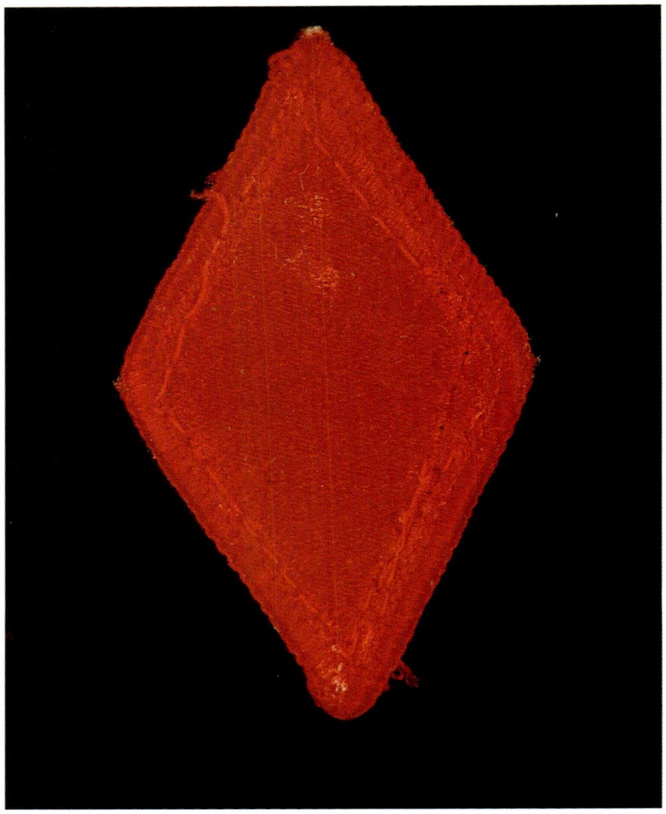

U.S. Army 1st Brigade, 5th Infantry Division (Mechanized)

U.S. Air Force 366th Tactical Fighter Wing
Da Nang, RVN

U.S. Naval Support Activity
Da Nang, RVN

DEFENSE DEPT. (MARINE CORPS) 1stMarDiv Vietnam Dec 67
U.S. Navy Construction Regiment "SeaBees" building Butler Building at Marine Aircraft Group-13, *Chu lai*, Republic of Vietnam.

Photograph from the author's personal collection of the Bob Hope Christmas USO show at the Marine Air Base *Chu Lai*, Republic of Vietnam.

U. S. NAVY Construction Battalion
(Seabees)

30th Naval Construction Regiment

38

Allies: Republic of Korea Marine Corps Serving with the III MAF

DEFENSE DEPT. PHOTO (MARINE CORPS) III MAF, Vietnam 9Mar67; (Photographer: LCpl ROMINE)
General KIM, Blue Dragon Brigade Commander, Republic of Korea Marine Corps, escorts U. S. Marine Corps Lieutenant General Victor H. KRULAK from a briefing at the Blue Dragon Headquarters, 15 miles south of *Chu Lai*,, RVN.

Republic of Korea Marine Corps

2nd Brigade, ROK Marines
19 Oct 1965 - February 1972

" Republic of Korea Marine Corps"

"2nd Battalion, ROK Marines"

39

Vintage Marine Corps Insignia
World War I and II Era

HEADQUARTERS MARINE CORPS - Photograph of Field 9, (June 12, 1918), Belleau Wood, France June 12, 1918. Bundy to Pershing: "...Approximately 250 prisoners, including 3 Officers, have been taken, and a number of machine guns and the 7 inch trench mortar."

5th Marine Regiment circa 1918 (WWI)
Marine 4th Infantry Brigade, U.S. Army 2nd
Division, American Expeditionary Force

6th Marine Regiment circa 1918 (WWI)
Marine 4th Infantry Brigade, U.S. Army 2nd
Division, American Expeditionary Force

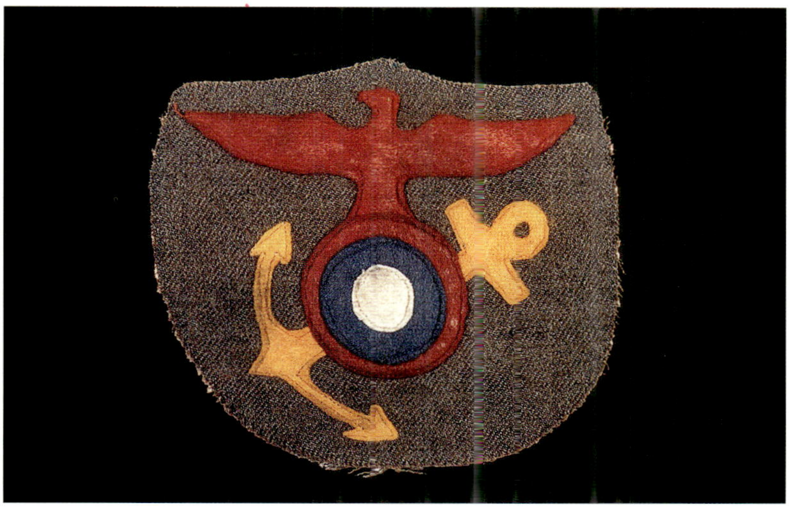

U.S. Marine Corps 1st Aviation Force
circa 1918 (WWI)

U.S. Marine Corps First Raider Battalion
circa 1945 (WWII)

40

Additional U.S. Marine Corps Unit Insignia

(unauthorized and unofficial "in-country" (Theater) made RVN

Personal photograph of Sergeant Don "Tex" DORSEY (Austin, Texas) as a Scout Sniper with the 1st Marine Division, 1st Marine Regiment in September 1969. The weapon carried is a USMC M40 medium-heavy, bull-barreled, bolt-action Remington 700 fitted with a green-body 3x9 variable Redfield scope. The rifle holds 5 rounds (1 in the chamber and 4 in the fold-out magazine). The location is a formerly *Viet Cong* (Communist) controlled area of southern I Corps called "Dodge City," 20 miles south of *Da Nang* in the *Quang Nam* Province, RVN.

U. S. Marine Corps - Official Seal

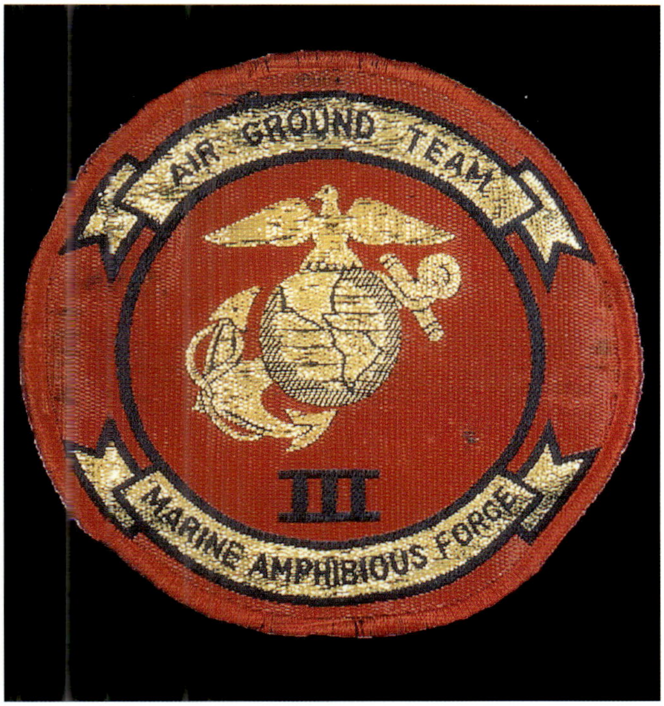

III MAF Air Ground Team

1st Mar Div, Vietnam

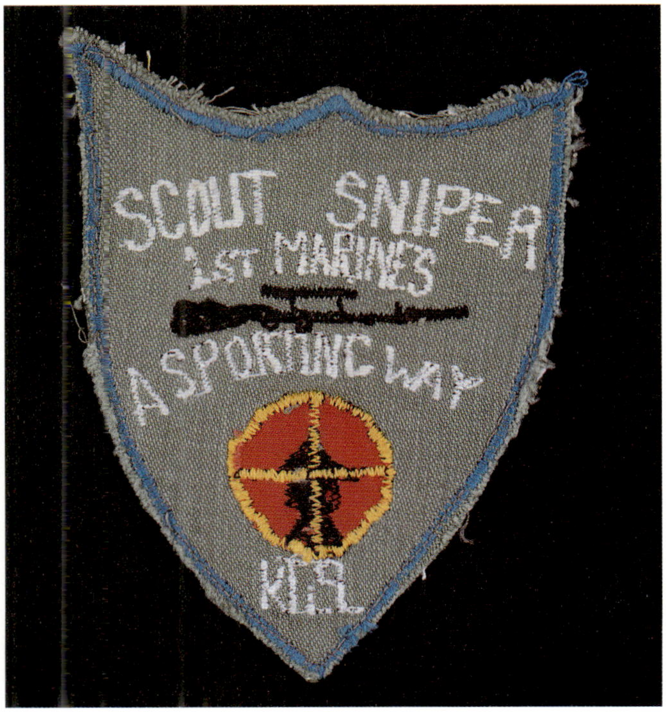

1st Marines, Scout Sniper Platoon

1st Marines, Scout Sniper (Recon)

1st Battalion, 1st Marine Regt

3rd Battalion, 1st Marine Regt

1st Bn 5th Marine Regt, Reconnaissance

2nd Bn 3d Marine Regt

2nd Bn 3d Marine Regt

9th Marine Regiment

2nd Battalion, 9th Marine Regt

2nd Battalion, 26th Marine Regiment

Task Force X-Ray
PUC 1Jan-2Mar68

2nd Battalion, 9th Marine Regt

1st Tank Battalion

3rd Motor Transport Battalion

3rd Motor Transport Battalion

9th Engineer Battalion

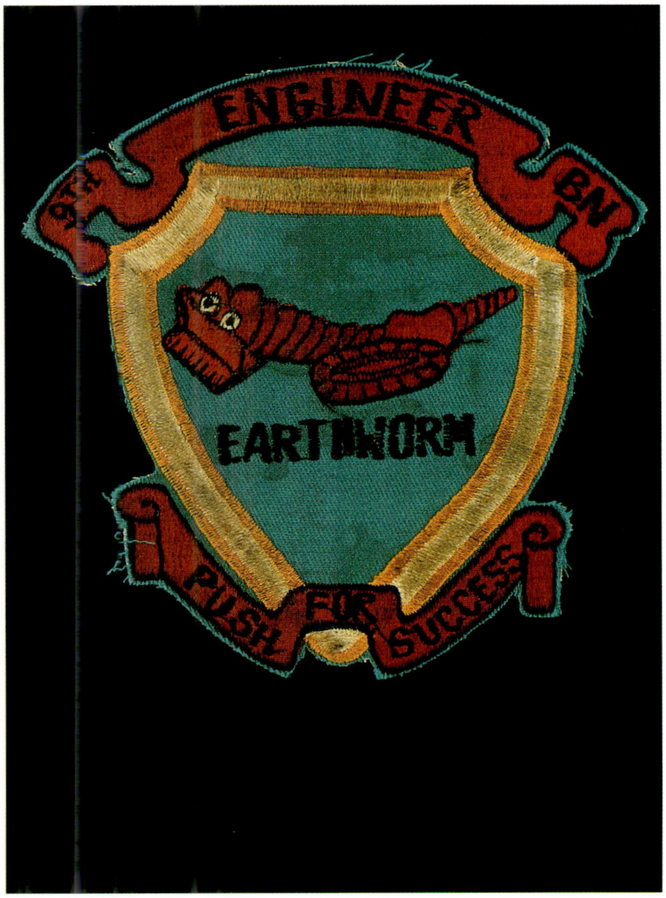

9th Engineer Battalion

3rd Marine Division
Reconnaissance

3rd Reconnaissance Battalion

U.S. Marine Corps Parachute Insignia

"Unauthorized Recon Death Wing"

USMC RECONDO
"Qualification Insignia"

3rd Service Battalion
MUC 12Mar65-30Jun69

Right: **Doc Charlies**
U. S. Navy Corpsman

MARS (Military Affiliate Radio Station)
U. S. Marine Corps' "HAM" Radio Operators

M-50 Anti-Tank Assault Vehicle "ONTOS"

Clockwise from Above Left:
U. S. Marine Corps Air Wing
"Snoopy" Flying Ace
HMM-163
HMM-163
HMM-261

HMM-262

HMM-262

HMM-263

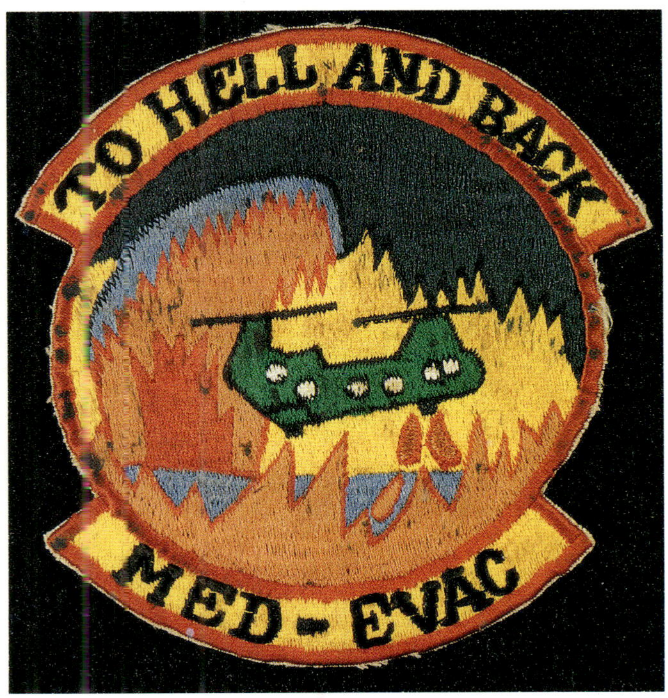

HMM-263

HMM-361

HMM-361

HMM-362

HMM-362

HMM-362

HMM-363

HMM-363

HMM-363

HMM-364

HMM-364

HMM-364

HMM-365

HMM-365

HMM-365

HMM-365

HMH-462

HMH-463

HMH-463

HMH-463

HMH-463

CH-46 Squadron

CH-46 Squadron

VMO-6 "Ordnance"

TAC(A) Hunting Club

HMM-165

HMM-165

Air Support Radar Team

Forward Air Control

41

Shoulder Scrolls and "Beer Can" Pocket Emblems

Sentry Dog Handler
Shoulder Scroll

"Marines Never Die..."
Shoulder Scroll

"IHTFP"
Shoulder Scroll

Rock Pile Combat Base
Shoulder Scroll

2nd Battalion 7th Marine Regiment
Pocket Emblem

1st Marine Reconnaissance
Pocket Emblem

3rd Medical Battalion
Pocket Emblem

1st Marine Division- Vietnam
Pocket Emblem

U.S. Marine Corps Aircraft Squadron Abbreviated Designations

Aircraft squadrons are assigned alphabetic designations based upon the type of aircraft in the squadron and the mission of those aircraft. The alphabetic designation also indicates the military service within which the squadron operates.

a. The first letter of the designation indicates the aircraft class:

V =	**Airplane/fixed-wing**
H =	Rotor craft/helicopter

b. The second letter of a squadron designation represents the operating service:

M =	**Service**	**(U. S. Marine Corps)**

c. Subsequent letters designate the general aircraft category and indicate the mission the squadron performs and special capabilities it may possess:

A:	**Attack**	**(AW): All-Weather**
B:	Composite	
F:	Fighter	
G:	Aerial Refueller	
O:	Observation	
P:	Tactical Reconnaissance	
Q:	Tactical Electronic Warfare	
R:	Transport	
T:	Training	
H:	Heavy Lift (Helicopter)	
M:	Medium Lift (Helicopter)	
L:	Light Lift (Helicopter)	
X:	Experimental/Special Mission	

Map of Southeast Asia with Military Regions of South Vietnam

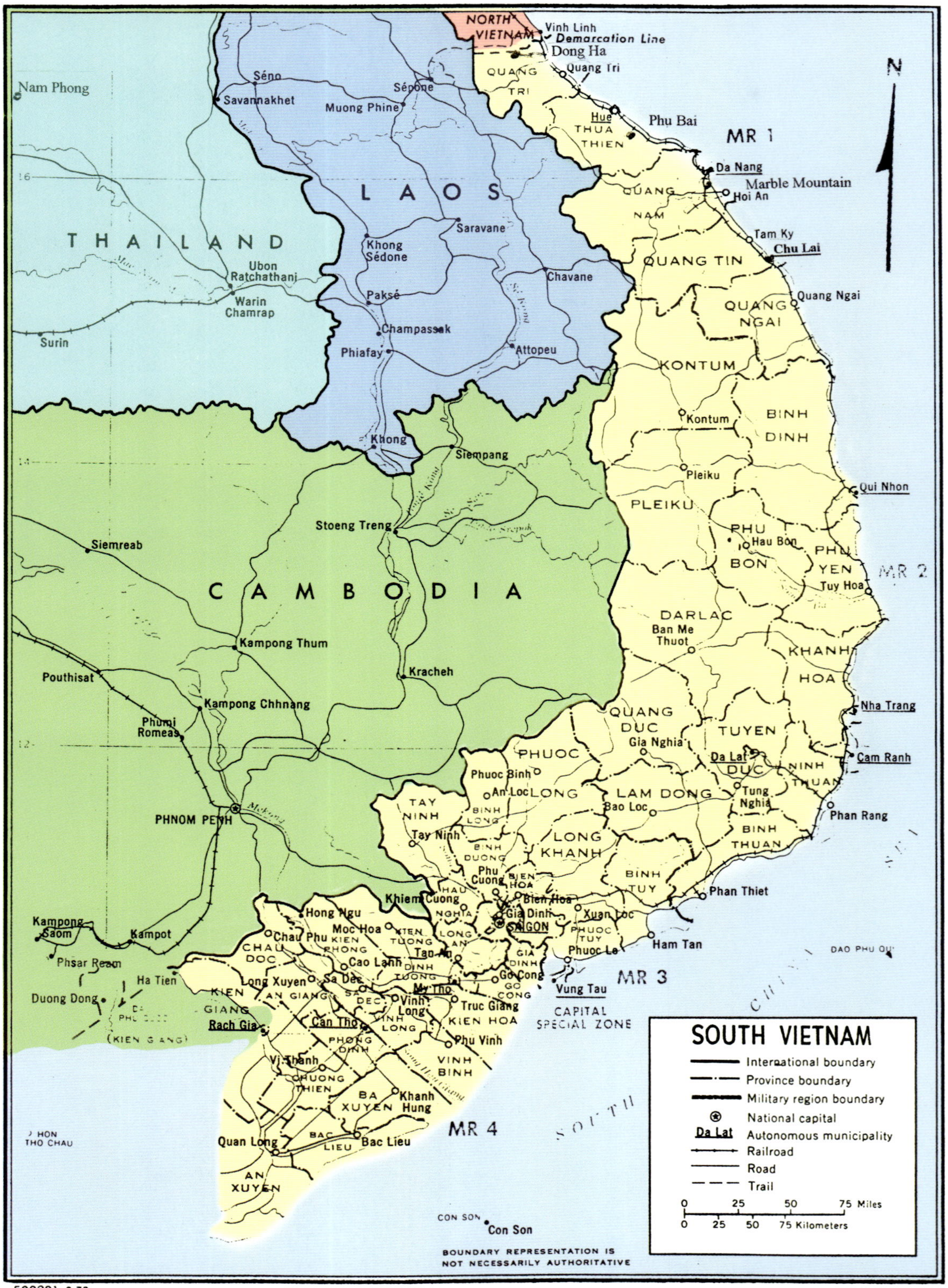

500201 2-73

Gossary of Terms and Abbreviations

Abn: Airborne
ANGLICO: Air & Naval Gunfire Liaison Company
AmTrac: Amphibious Assault Vehicle
AO: Aerial Observer.
A-O: Area of operations
ARVN: Army of the Republic of Vietnam
ASRTs: Air Support Radar Team - Each team is equipped with the TPQ-10 radar course
Azimuth: A direction in a horizontal plane.
Beer Can: Locally produced "in country" stamped & painted thin medal badge
Bird Dog: A light fixed-wing observation aircraft (O-1A).
BLT: Battalion Landing Team
Bn: Battalion
Btry: Battery
C's: C-rations or combat rations. Canned meals for field use.
CAF: Combined Action Force
CAP: Combined Action Platoon
Capt: Captain
CAR: Combat Action Ribbon
ChiCom: Chinese Communist
Cmdr: Commander
CO: Commanding Officer
Co: Company
Col: Colonel (0-6)
Cobra: The AH-IG attack helicopter
Combat Patrol: A patrol whose primary mission is to actively in combat with the enemy.
CONUS: Continental United States
Corpsman: U.S. Navy Medical Personnel serving with the U.S. Marine Corps
County Fair Operation: Search of village for suspected Viet Cong
CTZ: Corps Tactical Zone
Cpl: Corporal (E-4)
DET: Detachment - unit capable of self-sustained operations.
Div: Division
DMZ: Demilitarized Zone
Doc: Nax3' Corpsman (medical) personnel assigned to Marine units
DoD: Department of Defense
Dong: Vietnamese monetary unit; one piaster
DRV: Democratic Republic of Vietnam (North Vietnam)
Deuce: CH-53A Marines' twin rotor Heavy Lift Helicopter
FAC: Forward Air Control
FB: Firebase - Artillery firing position often secured by infantry
FIIU: Fleet Imagery Interpretation Unit
Fire fight: Skirmish between opposing units
FSB: Fire support Base
FSR: Force Service Regiment
GCM: General Court Martial
Gen: Gcncral (0-7, 0-8, 0-9, 0-10)
GySgl: Gunnery Sergeant (E-7)
Guerrilla: Armed combat element of the National Liberation Front
Hq: Headquarters
HQMC: Headquarters Marine Corps
Killer Team: Marine mobile ambush team
Klick: Short for Kilometer
LAAM: Light Antiaircraft Missile
LCpl: Lance Corporal (E-3)
LAW: M72 light antita~uk weapon
Lt: Lieutenant (0-1, 0-2)
LtCol: Lieutenant Colonel (0-5)
LZ: Landing Zone
MAB: Marine Amphibious Brigade
MAF: Marine Amphibious Force
Maj: Major (0-4)
MARHUK: Hunter-Killer Operations
MARS: Military Affiliated Radio Station
MEDCAP: Medical civic action program
Medevac: Medical evacuation by helicopter
MSGySgt: Master Gunnery Sergeant (E-9)
MSgt: Master Sergeant (E-8)
MAW: Marine Aircraft Wing
MACV-SOG: U.S. Army Military Assistance Command Vietnam - Studies and Observation Group
MCAF: Marine Corps Air Facility
MCAS: Marine Corps Air Station
MCB: Marine Corps Base

MEDCAP: Medical civic actions program
MEDEVAC: Medical evacuations - mission of Marine helicopter crews involved in rescuing wounded
MEF: Marine Expeditionary Force
MEU: Marine Expeditionary Unit
MMAF: Marble Mountain Air Facility
MOS: Mililary Occupation Specialty - four digit code for a specific job type (*eg*. 031 l-Infantryman)
MP: Military Police
MPC: Military Payment Certificate (U.S. Currency - Legal tender in a combat zone)
MUC: Meritorious Unit Commendation
NCO: Noncommissioned Officer (*eg*. E-4 to E-5)
NJP: Non-Judicial Punishment
NUC: Navy Unit Commendation
NVA: North Vietnamese Army
OP: Observation Post
0-1, 01C: Light single engine aircraft for forward air control and reconnaissance
PFC: Private First Class (E-2)
Pig: M-50 "Ontos" antitank assault vehicle
Pit: Plaloon
Prick: Nickname for the PRC-25 lightweight field radio
PUC: Presidential Unit Citation
Pvt: Private (E-l)
R & R: Rest-and-recreation vacation taken during one's one-year tour in Vietnam.
Recon: Reconnaissance "Snoop & Poop" Intelligence Information gathering
Regt: Regiment
REINF: Reinforced
lILT: Regimental Landing Team ROKs: Republic of Korea soldiers and marines
RPG: Rocket Propelled Grenade
RTII: Rotation tour date
RTO: Radio telephone operator
RVN: Republic of Vietnam
SAM: Surface to Air Missile
SAR: Search and Rescue
Seabees: Naval Construction engineers
Sgt: Sergeant (E-5)
SgtMaj: Sergeant Major (E-9)
SLICK: A Huey helicopter with no mounted guns.
SNCO: Staff Non-commissioned Officer (*eg*. E-6 to E-9)
SP: Self Propelled
SPCM: Special Court Martial
Sperm: Marine light observation helicopter
Sqd: Squad
Sqdn: Squadron
SSgt: Staff Sergeant (E-6)
SU: Sub Unit
TAC(A): Tactical Air Controller (Airborne)
TAORs: Tactical Areas of Responsibility
Tet: Chinese New Year Holiday period
TF: Task Force
UN: United Nations
Unit: Any military force having a prescribed organization
Utilities: Marine slang for combat fatigues
VC: Viet Cong (Victor Charles) Communist Forces - National Liberation Front
Victor Charlie: Phonetic alphabetization of V. C.
VMCJ: Composite Reconnaissance & Electronic Countermeasure Squadron
VMGR: Marine Aerial Refueller Transport Squadron
V/STOL: Vertical/Short Take-Off and Landing Aircraft
XO: Executive Officer, a unit's second in command

Unit Cross Reference Index

THE MARINES
HAVE LANDED

How to Use this Book

It is the author's intention to present at least one example of each U.S. Marine Corps unit insignia with service in the Republic of Vietnam down to Battalion and Squadron levels in a Order of Battle format on pages one through one hundred-ten. The reader must keep in mind that a particular unit insignia pictured in this book is not necessarily intended to be representative of any particular unit's entire period of service in Vietnam, but only one example of possibly many. Since individual unit insignia for Marine Corps' ground units, such as shoulder sleeve insignia, were not authorized for wear on the uniform, a particular design of an "in-country" made unit insignia was not documented by Headquarters Marine Corps. A unit's insignia could very well change in design, color, or pattern many times with a particular unit's service in the Republic of Vietnam.

Prices listed are based on the author's experience and are presented as a guide for informational purposes only. No one is obligated in any way to buy, sell, or trade according to these prices. The insignia's condition, rarity, and demand, as well as the reader's desire to own determine the actual value. No offer to buy or sell at the prices listed is intended or made. Buying and selling is conducted at the consumer's risk. Use of this book is with the understanding that the author, the publisher, and anyone connected with this work assume no liability for any losses suffered as a result of referring to, or any typographical errors contained in this book. All value estimates are presented in U.S. dollars. Keep in mind that the Latin term *"Caveat Emptor"* (let the buyer beware) are watch words for the serious collector to live by. True too for the collector of U.S. Marine Corps insignia of the Vietnam era. Arm yourself with this book as a handy reference, and most importantly, have fun collecting these unit representations of the Marine Corps' proud history.

The unit citations listed, as awarded to a particular Division, Regiment, or Battalion, are only a small sample of the awards earned. Unit citations such as the Presidential Unit Citation (PUC), Navy Unit Citation (NUC), and Meritorious Unit Commendation (MUC) will have the inclusive dates of the award. For a complete record of a Company or Platoon's unit awards refer to the Navy & Marine Corps Awards Manual by logging onto the internet and searching for NAVMC 2922.

Value Guide Reference Embroidered Unit Insignia

Values	**Position**	**Condition Description**
A Up to $50.00	**T** = top of page	**Mint:** As issued. Crisp and clear design.
B $51.00 to $100.00	**B** = bottom of page	**Excellent:** As issued with little visible wear.
C $101.00 to $250.00	**R** = right side of page	**Good:** Average wear, but clean and presentable.
D $251.00 to $500.00	**L** = left side of page	**Fair:** Shows a lot of use and lightly soiled.
E $501.00 to $1,000.00		**Poor:** Very Worn, with some fraying and fading.

VALUE GUIDE

Page	Position	Value	Page	Position	Value	Page	Position	Value
10	M	B	29	TR	B	47	TR	B
11	TL	C	29	BL	B	47	BL	g
11	TR	B	29	BR	A	47	BR	B
11	BL	E	31	TI,	A	50	TL	B
11	BR	A	31	TR	A	50	TR	A
12	TL	A	31	BI.	B	52	TL	A
12	TR	A	31	BR	B	52	TR	B
12	B	D	33	TL	B	52	BL	A
13	TL	B	33	TR	A	52	BR	B
13	TR	B	33	BL	B	54	TL	B
13	BL	B	33	BR	A	54	TR	B
13	BR	A	35	TL	B	54	BL	B
15	TL	B	35	TR	B	54	BR	B
15	TR	B	35	BL	B	56	T	B
15	BL	A	35	BR	B	56	B	B
15	BR	A	36	TL	B	58	T	B
17	TL	B	36	TR	C	58	B	C
17	TR	A	36	BL	A	59	TL	C
17	BL	B	36	BR	A	59	TR	A
17	|gR	B	37	TL	A	59	BL	B
19	TL	B	37	TR	B	59	BR	C
19	TR	C	37	BL	A	61	TL	C
19	BL	B	37	BR	B	61	TR	B
19	BR	A	39	TL	B	63	TL	B
21	TL	B	39	TR	B	63	TR	B
21	TR	A	39	BL	A	63	BL	A
21	BL	B	39	BR	A	63	BR	A
21	BR	A	41	TL	A	65	T	B
23	TL	B	41	TR	B	65	B	A
23	TR	A	41	BL	A	66	C	B
23	BI,	B	41	BR	A	68	TI	A
23	BR	A	42	TL	A	68	TR	B
25	TL	B	42	TR	B	68	BL	A
25	TR	C	42	BI,	B	68	BR	A
25	BL	B	42	BR	B	69	TL	B
25	BR	A	44	TL	A	69	TR	A
27	TL	A	45	TL	A	69	BL	A
27	TR	B	45	TR	A	69	BR	B
27	BL	A	45	BL	A	70	TL	A
27	BR	B	45	BR	B	70	TR	A
29	TL	A	47	TL	C	71	C	A

Page	Position	Value
72	T	A
72	B	A
73	C	B
74	TL	B
74	TR	B
75	C	A
76	TL	A
76	TR	A
76	BL	B
76	BR	A
77	C	A
78	TR	A
78	TL	B
78	B	A
79	C	A
80	TL	A
80	TR	B
82	TL	B
82	TR	A
82	BL	A
82	BR	A
83	TL	A
83	TR	A
83	BL	A
83	BR	A
84	TL	B
84	TR	B
84	BL	B
84	BR	B
85	TL	B
85	TR	A
85	BL	A
85	BR	A
86	TL	B
86	TR	I3
86	BL	B
86	BR	A
87	TL	A
87	TR	A
87	BL	A
87	BR	A
89	TL	B
89	TR	B
89	BL	B
89	BR	B
90	TL	B
90	TR	B
90	BL	A
90	BR	C
91	TL	A
91	TR	A
91	BL	A
91	BR	B
92	TL	C
92	TR	A
92	BL	A
92	BR	A
94	TL	A
94	TR	A
94	BL	B
94	BR	B
95	T	B
5	B	C
96	T	B
96	B	B
98	TL	A
98	TR	B
98	BL	A
98	BR	A
99	TL	A
99	TR	A
99	BL	A
99	BR	C
100	TL	A
100	TR	A
100	BL	A
100	BR	A
101	TL	A
101	TR	A
101	BL	A
101	BR	B
102	TL	A
102	TR	A
102	BL	A
102	BR	A
104	TL	A
104	TR	A
104	BL	A
104	BR	A
105	TL	A
105	TR	A
105	BL	B
105	BR	A
106	TL	A
106	TR	A
106	BI.	A
106	BR	B
107	T	B
107	B	B
108	T	B
108	B	B
110	TL	A
110	TR	A
110	BL	B
110	BR	B
111	T	A
111	1~	B
112	T	B
112	B	A
113	T	A
113	B	A
114	T	B
114	B	B
115	TL	B
115	TR	A
116	T	B
116	B	A
117	T	B
117	B	B
118	T	C
118	B	A
120	TL	B
120	TR	A
120	BL	A
120	BR	A
121	TL	A
121	TR	B
121	BL	A
121	BR	A
122	TL	C
122	TR	A
122	BL	A
122	BR	A
123	TL	A
123	TR	A
123	BL	B
123	BR	B
124	TL	A
124	TR	A
124	BL	A
124	BR	A
125	TL	C
125	TR	C
125	BL	C
125	BR	B
128	TL	A
128	TR	A

Page	Position	Value
128	BL	C
128	BR	C
129	T	B
129	B	B
130	T	A
130	B	A
132	TL	A
132	TR	A
132	BL	B
132	BR	B
133	TL	C
133	TR	A
133	BL	A
133	BR	A
135	TL	B
135	TR	B
137	TL	A
137	TR	A
139	T	A
139	B	A
140	T	A
140	B	A
142	TI~	B
142	TR	A
142	BL	A
142	BR	A
143	TL	B
143	TR	A
143	BL	A
143	BR	A
144	TL	B
144	TR	A
144	BL	C
144	BR	B
145	TL	A
145	TR	B
145	BL	A
145	BR	A
146	TL	C
146	TR	I3
146	BL	A
146	BR	B
147	TL	A
147	TR	A
147	BL	C
147	BR	B
148	TL	A
148	TR	A
148	BL	A
148	BR	A
149	TL	B
149	TR	A
149	BL	C
149	BR	C
150	TL	A
150	TR	A
150	BL	A
150	BR	A
151	TL	B
151	TR	A
151	BL	A
151	BR	A
152	TL	B
152	TR	B
152	BL	A
152	BR	13
153	TL	B
153	TR	A
153	BL	B
153	BR	B
154	TL	A
154	TR	A
154	BL	A
154	BR	B
155	TL	A
155	TR	A
155	BL	A
155	BR	A
156	TL	A
156	TR	A
156	BL	A
156	BR	A
157	TL	A
157	TR	A
157	BL	A
157	BR	A

Acknowledgments

Aiello, Ron 1st Scout Dog Pit; Burlington, NJ
Anderson, James
Armstrong, Victory, A., Maj General, USMC
Arciaga. "'Ace"; Oceanside, CA
Arthur, Gregg, Scottsdale, Arizona
Badger, Don, Gardner, Kansas
Bamford, L. R.; Las Vegas, Nevada
Banner, Michael T.; Oklahoma City, Oklahoma
Becker, S.; Dayton, Ohio
Beyer, Jaules J.
Birdsong, Neal L.; Gary, Indiana
Blaydes, E.C.
Blanchard, Clint; Niceville, FL
Blume, Richard, Iron Station, N.C.
Bongard, P.
Bonsoa. C.S.: Captain USMC
Bowers, M.J. Hospitalman 2"a, USN
Brooker, Gerald
Brooks, Bill
Broom, W.J. Gysgt USMC Ret.; Eureka, MT
Brown, FI Lauderdale, Florida
Carlson, Rod
Cartwright, Michael
Castro, Bill
Cohen, Ronald; U.S. Army, Lakewood, CA
Collins, J. J. GySgt USMC Ret. Costa Mesa, CA
Collins. Bill D.
Comey. C.K.; Sgt Major, USMC
Cook, R.
Coughlin, Lloyd
Cowan, William "Bill"; Lt Colonel USMC Ret.
Cullen, Larry
Curtis, Charles
Curtis. George: MstGySgt USMC Norwood, MA
Davis, Tim: Paso Robles, California
Deverick, Ron, Darien, Illinois
Dorsey, Don; Austin, Texas
Dunne, Thomas M.; Ellicott City, Maryland
Endo Jr., Rex K.; Iwakuni, Japan
Edens. Charles; Tulsa, Oklahoma
Fister, Dennis,
Feickert, P. R.
England, Stephen; Clinton, Oklahoma
Fagan, David: Monroeville, PA
Focks, Burnell; Guymon, Oklahoma
Fries, Ralph J. CWO-3 USN Ret.
Gass, Kenneth; Tulsa, Oklahoma
Gailbrath, Stephen; SSgt USMCNorman, OK
Gesswein Jr., Forrest F. Baltimore, Maryland
Ghanberry, Bob
Gibbs, Larry, Gering, Nebraska
Gilbert, James A.
Gladding, Orval, Cathedral City, California
Grams, Jay
Hall, L.S.
Haney, Robert J.; Mounds, Oklahoma
Harding, J.E.
Hare, Ronald; Mobile, Alabama
Heim, Russell F
Henry, Robert
Holman Jr., Arthur F. Marinette, MI
Holmberg, Eugene "Mule," Oceanside, CA
Hmnpert, D.E. 1sT Lieutenant USMC
Huly, George; Oceanside, California
Hughes, Gary; Anaheim, California
Hyatt, Mike; Candler, North Carolina
Judd, Randy; USN 30th NCR; Bethel Park, PA
Keating, Daniel; Lt Col USMC Ret., Tulsa, OK
Keith, Wes
Kelly Jr. Clement V.
Kenny, Eric; Sullivan, Illinois
Kim, Yung Soo; 1st Bn 2nd Bde R.O.K. Marine Corps
Koski, J.A.; lstSgt USMC Ret., Winchester, TN
Kruger, Gene
LaFountaine, Norm; Mattapoisett, MA
Larsen, Arthur A.
Latina, Sal
Leap, Michael; Blue Springs, MI
Leavy, H.F. CHC, Captain, U. S. Navy
Lucero, Richard R
Mastice, Joe
Maurer, Don
McConville, Joseph. "Mac"; Oceanside, California
McCracken, P.E. 1st Lieutenant USMC
McGrogan, Don
McKnight, Ron
Melton, William R. LtCol USMC Ret. Oklahoma City, OK
Miller, D.E. "Dano"; Lakeland, Florida
Moilers, Richard
Moon, Michael M.; Corporal USMC, Long Beach, CA

Moore, R. H.; Lt Colonel USMC Ret. McAllen, TX
Moran, Mike; Hoffman Estates, Illinois
Miscazak, Ed: South Surburan, Illinois
Murtha, Gary
Nardolillo, Peter C.; Albany, New York
Nastri, Tom; Costa Mesa, California
Nichols Jr., Don; Ralston, Nebraska
Noyles, P. M.; Lakeland, Florida
Nguyen, Mack; Garden Grove, California
Olivarri, John X. Houston, Texas
O'Neill, Bill
Pace, Jackie H
Parker, Gary; Toms River, New Jersey
Payne, Celia; MGySgt USMC Ret.
Povick, Nicholas M.; Elgin, Illinois
Rising, Barry L.;Danville, VA
Ross, Art
Roiusieau, Keith M.
Ruffini, John; Captain USMC; San Diego, CA
Russell, Richard; Col USAF, Laguna Nigel, CA
Sams, Richard, Anaheim, California
Sargent, Michael, Pinellas Park, Florida
Sawyer, Charles; Oklahoma Cily, OK
Scovel, Elizabeth J. LCpl USMC, Tulsa OK
Shaul, Richard D. Pickford, MI
Sisk. Michael D.; Baltimore, Maryland
Smith, Charles F. Lieutenant Colonel USMC
Spear, Dann; Marysville, California
Speight, R. J.
Street, William R., Cpl, U.S. Army Haleiwa, HI
Strout, Clifford
Steigelman, Herbert
Suazo, Richard H.; Hayward, California
Taft, John, North Merrick, New York
Thomas, M.J.; Grinnell, Iowa
Thurmond III, Joseph, Capt USMC Oceanside, CA
Torosian, John D. CWO, USMC
Traino Sr., Ronald; Fulton, NY
Udell, Dr. Donald PhD; Oklahoma City, OK
Walker, Audrey, York, PA
Ward, Charles (Chuck);Pleasant City, OH
Wean, Doug "Doc"
White, Bob
Whirr, Bob; Sib Stone Gap, VA
Wilder, R.V. 1st Sentry Dog Plt Cmdr; Round Rock, TX
Wilson, Julia A. Esquire, Edmond, Oklahoma

Marine Corps Historical Center
Bldg. #58, Washington Navy Yard
Washington, DC 20374-0580

Headquarters United States Marine Corps
Museums Branch
2014 Anderson Ave
Quantico, Virginia 22134-5002

First Marine Division Association
14325 Willard Rd, Ste #107
Chanlilly, VA 20151-2110

Third Marine Division Association, Inc.
P.O. Box 254
Chalfort, PA 18914-0254

Marine Corps Research Center
J.C. Breckinridge Library
H & S Bn - Code TUO5RL
Quantico, VA 22134-5010

United States Marine Corps
Heritage Foundation
P. O. Box 998
Quantico, VA 22134-0420

National Archives and Records
Administration
Still Picture Branch, NWCS, Rm 5360
8601 Adelphi Road
College Park, MD 20740-6001

1St Marine Aircraft Wing Assn.
Vietnam Service
PO Box 7240
Freeport, N.Y. 11520

Department of the Navy
Naval Historical Center (CUP)
805 Kidder Breese Street SE
Washington Navy Yard, DC 20374-5060

Museum of the Forgotten Warrior
5865 "A" Road
Maolsville, CA 95901
Curator/Founder Dann Spear

U.S. Marine Corps
Coordinating Council of Oklahoma, Inc.
1420 Evergreen Circle
Midwest City, OK 73110
Website: www.oklahomamarines.org

Bibliography

U.S. Marines in Vietnam 1965, The Landing and the Buildup, History and Museums Division Headquarters, U. S. Marine Corps, Washington, D.C. 1978

U.S. Marines in Vietnam, 1966, An Expanding War, History and Museums Division Headquarters, U. S. Marine Corps, Washington, D.C. 1982

U.S. Marines in Vietnam, 1967, Fighting the North Vietnamese, History and Museums Division Headquarters, U. S. Marine Corps, Washington, D.C. 1984

U.S. Marines in Vietnam, January-May 1968, History and Museums Division Headquarters, U. S. Marine Corps, Washington, D.C.

U.S. Marines in Vietnam, June-December 1968, History and Museums Division Headquarters, U. S. Marine Corps, Washington, D.C.

U.S. Marines in Vietnam, 1969, High Mobilit~ and Stand Down, History and Museums Division Headquarters, U. S. Marine Corps, Washington, D.C. by Charles Smith. 1989

U.S. Marines in Vietnam, 1970-1971, Vietnamization and Redeployment, History and Museums Division Headquarters, U. S. Marine Corps, Washington, D.C. by Graham A. Cosmas and Lt Col Terronce R. Murray, 1986

U.S. Marines in Vietnam, 1973-1975, The Bitter End, History and Museums Division Headquarters, U. S. Marine Corps, Washington, D.C. by George R. Dunham, *et al,* 1990.

Ambassadors in Green, Leatherneck Association, Inc., Washington, D.C. 1971.

Chronology ofIII MAF Buildup in RVN January 1965- May 1971, TAB 410-10, Marine Corps Command Center.

The Battle Standard of the U. S. Marine Corps, NAVMC 2637, Historical Division Headquarters, U. S. Marine Corps. Washington, D. C. 2000.

The Sea Tiger, Newspaper article, U.S. Marine Corps' **III** Marine Amphibious Force publication, Republic of Vietnam, 1971.

United States Marine Corps Award Manual, NAVMC 2922, 21 Apr 2002.

USMC Aviation Patches 1947-2002., Disk #1 Fixed Wing & Support Units, by Eugene S. Holmberg, 2002.

USMC Aviation Patches 1947-2002., Disk #2 Helicopter, STOL & Support Units, by Eugene S. Holmberg, 2003.

Vietnam Order of Battle, by Shelby L. Stanton, U.S. News Books, Washington, D.C., 1981.

DEFENSE DEPT. PHOTO (MARINE CORPS) 3dFSR, FMFPac (1972)
"Private First Class promotion ceremony of the author as a young Marine "lean green fighting machine" being handed a promotion warrant for his first "mosquito wing" (Private First Class) from H&S Company, Commanding Officer Captain D. P. EVANS with Company 1stSgt DIAZ in attendance."

About the Author

Eugene R. Wilson is a native Californian and graduated from John W. North High School, Riverside, CA. Upon completion of recruit training at MCRD San Diego, CA, and Schools Battalion at Camp Pendleton, CA, he was assigned to the 3rd Marine Division. Participated in counter-insurgency operations against Communist Forces in the Republic of Vietnam. Following a twelve month tour he was assigned to Marine Corps Air Station El Toro, CA, with Headquarters & Headquarters Squadron for duty at the Correctional Facility "Brig" as the Correctional Facility Supervisor. While stationed at MCAS, El Toro, participated in the Vietnamese Refugee Program and additional duty as a cross-country Prisoner Escort "chaser" for prisoners sentenced to the United States Discipline Barracks, Fort Leavenworth, Kansas. While stationed at El Toro completed two years of undergraduate work at Pepperdine University at Malibu, CA, as an Administration of Justice major.

Following his three years assignment at El Toro, assigned duty as a Marine Recruiter at the Inspector-Instructor Staff at the Marine Corps Reserve Center in Tulsa, Oklahoma. Upon completion of his two year tour as a Recruiter he was personally nominated by the Commanding Officer of the Recruiting Station for the Navy and Marine Corps Achievement Medal for superior performance. This award for a Recruiter was quite an honor to be earned in the mid 1970s considering the less than pro-national defense sentiment shared by the public at large. However, the real credit should go to the young patriotic men and women of Oklahoma for their love of God, Country, and Corps to sign up to defend our nation way before it was considered the "in" thing to do.

Upon completion active duty service transferred the Marine Corps Reserve at the 8" Howitzer (self propelled) Battery, Oklahoma City, OK and attended the University of Oklahoma, Norman OK on a full time basis. While with the Marine Reserve selected as one of three Reserve Staff Non-Commissioned Officers Marine Corps wide to augment with the Marine Corps' Officer Candidate School at (Brown Field) Quantico, Virginia for a period of ninety days as a Sergeant Instructor. The following summer, while still in college, selected for another ninety day period of temporary active duty as the Company Gunnery Sergeant and Chief of Security at the Marine Corps' Officer Candidate School northern most training site at Camp Upshur, Virginia during the debriefing of the Multi-Service Iranian Hostages Rescue Operation. Upon graduation from the University of Oklahoma with a Bachelor Degree in 1981, accepted for the United States Marine Corps' Officer Candidate School, 119th Officer Candidate Class and completed the Officers Basic School Course.

His vocational accomplishments include the Oklahoma University Police Department; Oklahoma Highway Patrol Academy; Orange County Sheriff Department Reserve, levels two and three; all culminating in action during the riots in Los

Angeles April, 1992, the night of the verdict, in support of the Los Angeles Police Department. His graduate educational endeavors include having attended Oklahoma City University's Masters in Criminal Justice Program intercession at Scotland Yard London, England; University of Oklahoma College of Law and even trying his hand at teaching in the Criminal Justice Department at the University of Central Oklahoma in Edmond, OK.

The author resides in Oklahoma City, Oklahoma, and is currently working as an Adjunct Professor of Criminal Justice for the U.S. Navy's College Program for Afloat College Education aboard the USS *Carl Vinson* (CVN-70). This vocation allows him the time, in between teaching assignments, to pursue his true advocation in continuing to chronicle this otherwise unheralded period of service of the U.S. Marine Corps in the Republic of Vietnam.

Christmas
3D MARINE DIVISION-VIETNAM